SPECTRUM

Math

Grade 3

Columbus, Ohio

Send all inquiries to:
School Specialty Publishing
8720 Orion Place
Columbus, OH 43240-2111

ISBN 0-7696-3703-5

6 7 8 9 10 HPS 11 10 09

Table of Contents Grade 3

Chapter 1 Adding and Subtracting 1- and 2-Digit Numbers (with renaming)

Chapter 2 Numeration through 100,000

Chapter 3 Adding and Subtracting 2- and 3-Digit Numbers (with renaming)

Chapter 4 Adding and Subtracting to 4 Digits (with renaming)

Chapter 5 Multiplying through 2 Digits by 1 Digit

Chapter 6 Division Facts through 81 ÷ 9

Chapter 7 Fractions

Chapter 8 Customary Measurement

Table of Contents, continued

NAME ______________________

Check What You Know

Adding and Subtracting 1- and 2-Digit Numbers (with renaming)

CHAPTER 1 PRETEST

Add.

	a	b	c	d	e
1.	23 + 19	17 + 5	37 + 42	11 + 75	81 + 9
2.	16 + 3	83 + 11	43 + 14	22 + 59	64 + 6
3.	30 + 23	7 + 25	9 + 36	18 + 25	93 + 2
4.	13 + 86	75 3 + 16	13 33 + 7	40 51 + 2	15 27 + 46

Subtract.

	a	b	c	d	e
5.	90 − 10	16 − 9	23 − 18	27 − 7	19 − 11
6.	57 − 16	84 − 23	16 − 11	25 − 5	62 − 19
7.	97 − 58	46 − 23	81 − 27	48 − 13	74 − 9
8.	32 − 24	73 − 12	65 − 30	70 − 20	23 − 8

NAME ____________________

Check What You Know

SHOW YOUR WORK

Adding and Subtracting 1- and 2-Digit Numbers (with renaming)

Solve each problem.

9. The florist has 63 roses and carnations. If she has 27 roses, how many carnations does she have?

The florist has ________ roses and carnations.

She has ________ roses.

The florist has ________ carnations.

9.

10. Bly has 43 pennies, 13 dimes, and 16 nickels. How many coins does she have in all?

Bly has ________ pennies.

She has ________ dimes.

She has ________ nickels.

Bly has ________ coins in all.

10.

11. There are 36 students in Cleveland's class this year. If 22 are girls, how many boys are in Cleveland's class?

There are ________ students in Cleveland's class.

There are ________ girls in his class.

There are ________ boys in his class.

11.

12. The store has 53 cases of apples and oranges in the storeroom. If there are 28 cases of apples, how many cases of oranges are there in the storeroom?

There are ________ cases of oranges in the storeroom.

12.

NAME ______________________

Lesson 1.1 Adding through 18

addend	3	→	Find the **3**-row.
addend	+ 8	→	Find the **8**-column.
sum	11	←	The sum is named where the 3-row and the 8-column meet.

8-column

Addend

3-row

Addend

+	0	1	2	3	4	5	6	7	8	9
0	0	1	2	3	4	5	6	7	8	9
1	1	2	3	4	5	6	7	8	9	10
2	2	3	4	5	6	7	8	9	10	11
3	3	4	5	6	7	8	9	10	11	12
4	4	5	6	7	8	9	10	11	12	13
5	5	6	7	8	9	10	11	12	13	14
6	6	7	8	9	10	11	12	13	14	15
7	7	8	9	10	11	12	13	14	15	16
8	8	9	10	11	12	13	14	15	16	17
9	9	10	11	12	13	14	15	16	17	18

Add.

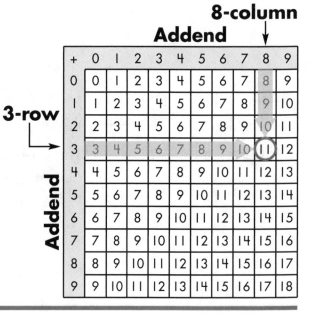

	a	b	c	d	e	f
1.	2 +3	7 +9	2 +5	1 +7	0 +3	9 +5
2.	7 +2	3 +3	9 +0	6 +5	0 +7	8 +5
3.	4 +3	2 +9	7 +7	5 +6	5 +9	0 +6
4.	0 +0	8 +3	8 +6	6 +1	5 +3	4 +8
5.	5 +2	3 +1	2 +4	8 +2	8 +8	3 +6
6.	4 +6	5 +0	3 +7	6 +9	9 +9	5 +7

NAME ____________________

Lesson 1.2 Subtracting through 18

minuend 12 →	Find the **12** in
subtrahend − 7 →	the **7**-column.
difference 5 ←	The difference is the number at the end of the row.

7-column

−	0	1	2	3	4	5	6	7	8	9
0	0	1	2	3	4	5	6	7	8	9
1	1	2	3	4	5	6	7	8	9	10
2	2	3	4	5	6	7	8	9	10	11
3	3	4	5	6	7	8	9	10	11	12
4	4	5	6	7	8	9	10	11	12	13
5	5	6	7	8	9	10	11	12	13	14
6	6	7	8	9	10	11	12	13	14	15
7	7	8	9	10	11	12	13	14	15	16
8	8	9	10	11	12	13	14	15	16	17
9	9	10	11	12	13	14	15	16	17	18

Subtract.

	a	b	c	d	e	f
1.	7 − 2	6 − 0	5 − 4	11 − 6	16 − 9	13 − 8
2.	6 − 3	9 − 6	5 − 2	8 − 0	18 − 9	9 − 7
3.	7 − 2	3 − 0	8 − 2	7 − 4	10 − 3	9 − 2
4.	4 − 0	3 − 2	9 − 3	13 − 5	13 − 8	8 − 4
5.	12 − 5	6 − 4	1 − 0	12 − 3	10 − 6	11 − 5
6.	3 − 1	4 − 3	9 − 1	5 − 1	8 − 7	14 − 8

NAME ____________________

Lesson 1.3 Adding 2-Digit Numbers (no renaming)

First, add the ones. Then, add the tens.

43	43	43	addend
+22	+22	+22	addend
	5	65	sum

22	addend
+16	addend
38	sum

First, add the ones.
Then, add the tens.

Add.

	a	b	c	d	e	f
1.	23 + 16	11 + 22	20 + 10	16 + 12	73 + 15	63 + 13
2.	10 + 17	18 + 30	13 + 14	32 + 51	81 + 11	34 + 21
3.	14 + 12	34 + 13	41 + 18	30 + 50	27 + 50	22 + 22
4.	18 + 41	13 + 42	12 + 44	31 + 17	27 + 42	31 + 38
5.	13 + 14	15 + 43	23 + 42	22 + 71	37 + 60	35 + 23
6.	10 + 43	73 + 20	86 + 13	52 + 13	42 + 26	32 + 45

NAME ______________________

Lesson 1.4 Subtracting 2-Digit Numbers (no renaming)

First, subtract the ones. Then, subtract the tens.

36	36	36	minuend
−23	−23	−23	subtrahend
	3	13	difference

Subtract.

	a	b	c	d	e	f
1.	23 − 12	86 − 22	93 − 71	30 − 10	92 − 11	48 − 16
2.	62 − 10	83 − 13	65 − 44	54 − 12	37 − 25	88 − 32
3.	86 − 45	92 − 70	89 − 62	75 − 62	88 − 44	90 − 60
4.	82 − 41	57 − 36	35 − 23	65 − 43	81 − 60	42 − 30
5.	60 − 30	46 − 25	92 − 81	86 − 32	57 − 36	29 − 13
6.	25 − 15	28 − 12	36 − 13	46 − 15	75 − 14	64 − 23

NAME ____________________

Lesson 1.5 Adding 2-Digit Numbers (with renaming)

Add the ones.
Rename 12 as 10 + 2.

Add the tens.

37 +25	7 + 5 12 or 10 + 2	1 37 +25 2	1 37 +25 62	addend addend sum

Add.

	a	b	c	d	e	f
1.	23 +18	76 +15	13 +77	36 +16	19 +62	29 +19
2.	27 +36	52 +39	36 +28	30 +50	56 +27	59 +13
3.	54 +27	53 +28	28 +17	13 +19	39 +17	56 +14
4.	62 +19	27 +18	26 +55	18 +13	72 +18	37 +17
5.	23 +57	29 +16	25 +16	38 +14	26 +28	76 +15
6.	29 +17	34 +27	43 +27	25 +26	48 +12	45 +46

NAME ____________________

Lesson 1.6 Subtracting 2-Digit Numbers (with renaming)

	Subtract the ones. Rename 52 as "4 tens and 12 ones."	Subtract the ones.	Subtract the tens.	
52 −19	$\overset{4\ 12}{\not{5}\not{2}}$ −19	$\overset{4\ 12}{\not{5}\not{2}}$ −19 3	$\overset{4\ 12}{\not{5}\not{2}}$ −19 33	minuend subtrahend difference

Subtract.

	a	b	c	d	e	f
1.	30 −22	22 −19	53 −28	41 −27	92 −56	86 −27
2.	83 −66	62 −56	51 −17	34 −15	46 −29	57 −38
3.	72 −37	82 −67	64 −18	86 −57	41 −16	53 −29
4.	24 −17	60 −20	86 −27	93 −26	52 −17	47 −28
5.	86 −38	45 −18	42 −19	96 −39	63 −27	87 −68
6.	53 −17	92 −45	86 −18	72 −17	63 −45	52 −13

NAME ____________________

Lesson 1.7 Adding Three Numbers

Add the ones. | Add the tens.

```
  23      3 \
  47      7 —   10                 1
 +16     +6    + 6                23       1
 ---     ---   ---                47      23   addend
                16 or 10 + 6     +16      47   addend
                                 ---     +16   addend
                                   6     ---
                                          86   sum
```

Add.

	a	b	c	d	e	f
1.	13 26 +45	7 29 +56	16 23 +25	27 7 +34	6 13 +29	10 30 +50
2.	22 31 +45	19 21 +32	29 16 +15	13 15 +25	42 21 + 8	26 23 +35
3.	11 30 +42	27 16 + 9	4 7 +8	34 16 +41	16 23 +35	29 31 +25
4.	82 5 + 9	33 47 +12	86 5 + 2	18 32 +16	46 29 +16	53 21 +15
5.	66 21 + 8	47 13 + 8	22 41 +28	23 15 +17	18 16 +24	23 35 +17

NAME ______________________

Lesson 1.8 Addition and Subtraction Practice

Add or subtract.

	a	b	c	d	e	f
1.	23 −10	76 +21	82 −19	16 7 +13	16 +35	76 −30
2.	20 +50	30 −13	16 13 +23	76 −43	87 −45	92 −79
3.	26 +58	96 −17	72 + 3	79 + 8	16 − 8	18 12 +42
4.	86 −19	77 +16	43 −29	16 + 7	82 −42	86 −39
5.	57 −43	9 +9	0 +30	41 −22	18 42 +13	18 +53
6.	81 −79	27 +34	86 +13	92 −36	37 −24	86 + 5

NAME ______________________

Lesson 1.9 Problem Solving

SHOW YOUR WORK

Solve each problem.

1. Philip has 52 marbles. His friend, Edgar, has 39 marbles. How many marbles do they have in all?

   Philip has __________ marbles.

   Edgar has __________ marbles.

   They have __________ marbles in all.

2. Susan has 3 cats. George has 23 fish. Maria has 2 birds. How many pets do they have together?

   Susan has __________ cats.

   George has __________ fish.

   Maria has __________ birds.

   Together they have __________ pets.

3. Mr. Williams' third-grade class has 27 students. Mrs. Nakagawa's third-grade class has 31 students. How many third-grade students are there?

   Mr. Williams has __________ students.

   Mrs. Nakagawa has __________ students.

   Together, there are __________ students.

4. There are 36 adults and 17 children at the movie theater. How many people are at the movie theater?

   There are __________ people at the movie theater.

5. Kyle has 77 baseball trading cards. If Omar gives Kyle 13 baseball trading cards, how many trading cards will Kyle have?

   Kyle will have __________ baseball trading cards.

1.

2.

3.

4.

5.

NAME ____________________

Lesson 1.10 Problem Solving

SHOW YOUR WORK

Solve each problem.

1. Mrs. Lopez has 32 rose bushes in her garden. If 14 are not blooming, how many are blooming?

Mrs. Lopez has ________ rose bushes in her garden.

There are ________ bushes that are not blooming.

There are ________ bushes that are blooming.

2. Tamika has 15 cousins. If 11 of her cousins are girls, how many of her cousins are boys?

Tamika has ________ cousins.

She has ________ cousins who are girls.

Tamika has ________ cousins who are boys.

3. There are 76 seats on the plane. There are 62 passengers on the plane. How many empty seats are on the plane?

There are ________ seats on the plane.

There are ________ passengers.

There are ________ empty seats on the plane.

4. There are 56 books on the bookshelf. If 39 are not mystery books, how many are mystery books?

There are ________ mystery books on the bookshelf.

5. My book has 38 pages in it. If there are 12 pages that have pictures, how many pages do not have pictures?

There are ________ pages in the book that do not have pictures.

1.

2.

3.

4.

5.

NAME ____________________

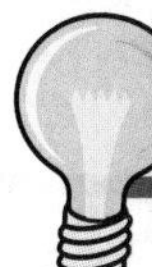

Check What You Learned

Adding and Subtracting 1- and 2-Digit Numbers (with renaming)

Add.

	a	b	c	d	e	f
1.	23 + 47	17 + 22	18 + 53	6 + 27	30 + 50	27 + 0
2.	86 + 12	63 + 29	13 + 37	47 + 23	19 + 29	63 + 21
3.	25 + 35	5 + 31	20 + 0	49 + 26	33 + 44	46 + 53
4.	86 + 5	75 + 6	13 + 12 + 23	63 + 19 + 8	11 + 22 + 33	16 + 32 + 11

Subtract.

	a	b	c	d	e	f
5.	93 − 5	76 − 13	82 − 45	67 − 41	14 − 12	63 − 0
6.	87 − 19	28 − 13	65 − 42	57 − 35	63 − 14	39 − 25
7.	46 − 23	80 − 20	65 − 9	92 − 45	99 − 35	86 − 19
8.	53 − 45	39 − 23	86 − 14	92 − 47	85 − 45	62 − 37

CHAPTER 1 POSTTEST

NAME ______________________

Check What You Learned

SHOW YOUR WORK

Adding and Subtracting 1- and 2-Digit Numbers (with renaming)

Solve each problem.

9. At an air show there were 32 airplanes in the sky. If 15 airplanes landed, how many were still in the sky?

There were ________ airplanes still in the sky.

10. One bag of rocks weighs 15 pounds. Another bag of rocks weighs 23 pounds. How much do both bags of rocks weigh?

Together, the bags of rocks weigh ________ pounds.

11. There were 46 people at the train station. 27 people got on the train. How many people are still at the train station?

There are ________ people still at the train station.

12. Sally has 32 cupcakes. She gave cupcakes to 16 people. How many cupcakes does she have left?

Sally has ________ cupcakes left.

13. The car dealer had 17 model cars. Yesterday, he sold 9 of the model cars. How many model cars does he have left?

The car dealer has ________ model cars left.

14. Beatrix had invited 26 people to her party. Only 9 people could not come to the party. How many people will be at Beatrix's party?

There will be ________ people at Beatrix's party.

9.
10.
11.
12.
13.
14.

NAME ______________________

Check What You Know

Numeration through 100,000

CHAPTER 2 PRETEST

Show the value of 5 in each number.

	a	b	c	d
1.	325	395,061	4,500	49,705
	______	______	______	______
2.	5,439	542,960	437,590	753
	______	______	______	______

What digit is in the place named?

	a	b	c	d
3.	5,764 tens	432 ones	5,940 thousands	631 hundreds
	______	______	______	______
4.	459,643 ten thousands	93,046 hundreds	9,764 tens	403,000 hundred thousands
	______	______	______	______

Write each number in expanded form.

	a	b	c	d
5.	596	40,321	170,018	90,431
	______	______	______	______
6.	73	987	5,041	803,731
	______	______	______	______

NAME ______________________

Check What You Know

Numeration through 100,000

Compare each pair of numbers. Write <, >, or =.

	a	b	c	d
7.	30 ___ 32	9 ___ 10	171 ___ 1,710	596 ___ 593
8.	43 ___ 27	30 ___ 30	16 ___ 13	960 ___ 431

Circle the greatest number.

	a	b	c	d
9.	32 14 96	17 21 17	191 25 460	43 57 21

Round each number to the place named.

	a	b	c	d
10.	543 tens ________	867 hundreds ________	479 tens ________	962 tens ________
11.	5,678 thousands ________	9,654 tens ________	7,432 hundreds ________	1,605 tens ________

SHOW YOUR WORK

Solve each problem.

12. Write the greatest number that you can write using the digits 5, 9, 8, and 1.

The largest number is ________.

13. Write the smallest number that you can write using the digits 7, 3, 2, and 2.

The smallest number is ________.

14. If Susana has 5 dimes and Rick has 13 dimes, who has the most dimes?

________ has the most dimes.

12.

13.

14.

NAME ____________________

Lesson 2.1 Understanding Place Value (to hundreds)

Use this chart to help you tell the value of each digit.

Hundreds	Tens	Ones
5	7	2
The value of 5 is 5 hundreds or 500.	The value of 7 is 7 tens or 70.	The value of 2 is 2 ones or 2.

The expanded form of a number is written as a sum showing the place values.

The expanded form of 572 is 500 + 70 + 2.

Show the value of 3 in each number.

	a	b	c	d
1.	324 300	135 _____	36 _____	513 _____

Name the value of the digit in the place named.

	a	b	c	d
2.	231 hundreds _____	63 ones _____	725 tens _____	123 tens _____
3.	691 tens _____	192 ones _____	23 tens _____	392 hundreds _____

Write each number in expanded form.

	a	b	c	d
4.	563 _____	92 _____	861 _____	153 _____
5.	252 _____	18 _____	65 _____	392 _____

NAME ______________________

Lesson 2.1 Problem Solving

SHOW YOUR WORK

Solve each problem.

1. Circle the expanded form that expresses 213.

100 + 20 + 3

200 + 30 + 1

200 + 10 + 3

300 + 20 + 3

2. Shawn has 325 dollars. If Shawn uses only hundreds, tens, and ones, write the number of each kind of bill that Shawn has.

He has __________ hundred-dollar bills.

He has __________ ten-dollar bills.

He has __________ one-dollar bills.

3. Adriana has two hundred-dollar bills and three ten-dollar bills. How much money does Adriana have?

The two hundred-dollar bills are worth __________ dollars.

The three ten-dollar bills are worth __________ dollars.

Since there are __________ one-dollar bills, the

ones place will have a __________.

Adriana has __________ dollars.

4. Bruce is playing with a set of base-ten blocks. He has 65 ten-blocks and 7 one-blocks. What is the value of his-blocks?

He can use __________ ten-blocks to represent

__________ hundred blocks.

The value of his blocks is __________.

1.

2.

3.

4.

NAME ____________________

Lesson 2.2 Understanding Place Value (to ten thousands)

7 2 , 3 5 6

ten thousands, thousands, hundreds, tens, ones

The 2 has a value of 2 thousands or 2,000.

The 7 has a value of 7 ten thousands or 70,000.

Show the value of 5 in each number.

	a	b	c	d
1.	75,032 5,000	51,232 ______	365 ______	12,354 ______

Which digit is in the place named?

	a	b	c	d
2.	562 ones ___ is in the ones place.	35,961 hundreds ___ is in the hundreds place.	35,462 ten thousands ___ is in the ten thousands place.	46,123 thousands ___ is in the thousands place.

Name the place of the underlined digit.

	a	b	c	d
3.	<u>3</u>6,542 ___ is in the __________ place.	96,<u>4</u>91 ___ is in the __________ place.	1<u>2</u>,331 ___ is in the __________ place.	<u>6</u>51 ___ is in the __________ place.

Write each number in expanded form.

	a	b	c	d
4.	50,631 ______________	12,560 ______________	963 ______________	43,561 ______________
5.	81,009 ______________	32,451 ______________	6,320 ______________	2,406 ______________

NAME ____________________

Lesson 2.2 Problem Solving

SHOW YOUR WORK

Solve each problem.

1. Write the place value name for each digit in the number 542.

   5 is in the __________ place.

   4 is in the __________ place.

   2 is in the __________ place.

2. Write the number described. 8 is in the tens place. The digit in the ones place is three less than the digit in the tens place. The digit in the hundreds place is one-half the digit in the tens place. The digit in the thousands place is one more than the digit in the tens place. The digit in the ten thousands place is the same as the digit in the tens place.

   ____ is in the ten thousands place.

   ____ is in the thousands place.

   ____ is in the hundreds place.

   ____ is in the tens place.

   ____ is in the ones place.

   The number is __________.

3. Using the digits 5, 9, 1, 2, and 6, write the smallest number possible.

   The smallest digit, ____, will be in the __________ place.

   The greatest digit, ____, will be in the __________ place.

   The smallest number possible using the digits 5, 9, 1, 2, and 6 is __________.

4. Circle the number represented by 30,000 + 200 + 3.

   30,233   32,300   30,203   32,003

1.

2.

3.

4.

NAME ______________________

Lesson 2.3 Understanding Place Value (to hundred thousands)

4 6 2 , 3 5 1

hundred thousands, ten thousands, thousands, hundreds, tens, ones

Show the value of 2 in each number.

	a	b	c	d
1.	203,471	123,459	11,204	713,452
	200,000	______	______	______

Which digit is in the place named?

	a	b	c	d
2.	531,462 hundred thousands	62,496 hundreds	92,963 thousands	423,541 ten thousands
	___ is in the hundred thousands place.	___ is in the hundreds place.	___ is in the thousands place.	___ is in the ten thousands place.

Name the place of the underlined digit.

	a	b	c	d
3.	<u>4</u>51,679	9<u>6</u>,451	1<u>0</u>8,709	65<u>2</u>,982
	___ is in the ______ place.	___ is in the ______ place.	___ is in the ______ place.	___ is in the ______ place.

Write each number in expanded form.

	a	b	c	d
4.	600,981	730,104	80,360	91,123
	______	______	______	______
5.	123,456	98,731	103,407	605,431
	______	______	______	______

NAME ______________________________

Lesson 2.3 Problem Solving

SHOW YOUR WORK

Solve each problem.

1. Write the number described:

0 is in the tens place, the thousands place, and the ten thousands place.

3 is in the ones place.

The digit in the hundreds place is three times the digit in the ones place.

The digit in the hundred thousands place is two times the digit in the ones place.

The number is ___ ___ ___, ___ ___ ___.

1.

2. Alicia has 6 stacks of cards. Each stack of cards has a value. She has 2 cards in her stack of hundred thousands value cards. She has 5 ten thousands value cards. She has 2 thousands value cards. She has 9 hundreds value cards. Her stacks of tens value cards and ones value cards have 5 cards each. Write Alicia's card stacks in expanded form.

___ hundred thousands

___ ten thousands

___ thousands

___ hundreds

___ tens

___ ones

Expanded form:

____

2.

3. Use the digits 3, 5, 7, 2, 9, and 1 to write the greatest number possible.

____

3.

4. Use the digits 3, 5, 7, 2, 9, and 1 to write the smallest number possible.

____

4.

NAME ____________________

Lesson 2.5 Rounding

The steps for rounding are:

1) Look one place to the right of the digit you wish to round.
2) If the digit is less than 5, leave the digit in the rounding place as it is, and change the digits to the right of the rounding place to zero.
3) If the digit is 5 or greater, add 1 to the digit in the rounding place, and change the digits to the right of the rounding place to zero.

Round 5,432 to the nearest thousand. 5 is in the thousands place. Look at the 4. Do not change the 5. 5,432 to the nearest thousand is 5,000.

Round each number to the nearest ten.

	a	b	c	d
1.	963 960	154 ______	186 ______	4,031 ______
2.	125 130	3,452 ______	8,657 ______	7,987 ______

Round each number to the nearest hundred.

	a	b	c	d
3.	8,765 ______	986 ______	3,250 ______	7,913 ______
4.	507 ______	1,349 ______	842 ______	4,370 ______

Round each number to the place named.

	a	b	c	d
5.	8,576 hundreds ______	1,930 thousands ______	364 tens ______	1,543 tens ______
6.	1,886 hundreds ______	765 tens ______	863 hundreds ______	86 tens ______
7.	451 tens ______	8,713 tens ______	472 hundreds ______	5,325 tens ______
8.	3,651 thousands ______	123 tens ______	486 tens ______	2,356 hundreds ______

NAME ____________________

Lesson 2.4 Greater Than, Less Than, or Equal To

Compare the numbers. Write <, >, or =.

< means "is less than." > means "is greater than." = means "is equal to."	If two numbers are not equal when comparing them, they are **unequal**. These comparisons are called **inequalities**.

Compare 36 and 92. Compare the value. Look at the biggest place value. In this case it would be the tens place. 3 tens is less than 9 tens.

36 "is less than" 92.

36 <u> < </u> 92

Compare 193 and 122. Compare the value. Look at the hundreds place. Since the hundreds place is the same in both, look at the tens place. 9 tens "is greater than" 2 tens.

193 <u> > </u> 122

Compare each pair of numbers. Write <, >, or =.

	a	b	c	d
1.	3,342 ___ 3,339	305 ___ 272	200 ___ 200	180 ___ 810
2.	352 ___ 357	75 ___ 70	186 ___ 286	910 ___ 910
3.	1,964 ___ 1,694	3,721 ___ 986	2,545 ___ 2,541	183 ___ 189

Circle the greatest number.

	a	b	c	d
4.	9,000 900 9	32 23 67	10 1,100 110	3 7 11
5.	25 27 17	86 54 16	80,001 80,100 810	323 232 131

SHOW YOUR WORK

Solve each problem.

6. Andy has 4 ten-dollar bills and 5 one-dollar bills. Sheila has 3 ten-dollar bills and 15 one-dollar bills. Henry has 8 ten-dollar bills and 4 one-dollar bills. Who has the same amount of money?

__________ and __________ have the same amount of money.

7. Enrique has 7 comic books. Adelina has 2 more comic books than Enrique. Susana has 4 fewer comic books than Enrique. Who has the most comic books?

__________ has the most comic books.

6.

7.

NAME ______________________

Check What You Learned

Numeration through 100,000

Show the value of 2 in each number.

	a	b	c	d
1.	32	250	10,251	92,054
	______	______	______	______
2.	629	4,527	27,531	43,592
	______	______	______	______

What digit is in the place named?

	a	b	c	d
3.	321 hundreds	5,412 tens	9,865 thousands	796 ones
	______	______	______	______

Name the place of the underlined digit.

	a	b	c	d
4.	7<u>5</u>,361	8,9<u>0</u>4	<u>8</u>65	98<u>7</u>
	___ is in the ________ place.	___ is in the ________ place.	___ is in the ________ place.	___ is in the ________ place.

Write each number in expanded form.

	a	b	c	d
5.	592	4,532	4,907	16,983
	______	______	______	______
6.	10,700	180,982	90,531	63
	______	______	______	______

CHAPTER 2 POSTTEST

NAME ______________________

Check What You Learned

Numeration through 100,000

Compare each pair of numbers. Write <, >, or =.

	a	b	c	d
7.	52 ___ 96	5 ___ 8	73 ___ 72	980 ___ 970

Circle the greatest number.

	a	b	c	d
8.	16 15 17	29 32 29	76 760 67	13 93 102

Circle the smallest number.

	a	b	c	d
9.	23 96 21	56 92 82	20 30 40	16 16 14

Round each number to the place named.

	a	b	c	d
10.	592 hundreds ______	86 tens ______	5,432 thousands ______	981 tens ______

SHOW YOUR WORK

Solve each problem.

11. What is the greatest number that you can write using the digits 0, 7, 4, 6, and 3?

The greatest number is ________.

12. Circle the number represented by 4,000 + 30 in expanded form.

400,030   404,330   4,030   4,303

13. Luke wants to buy a radio that costs 37 dollars plus sales tax. Round the cost of the radio to the tens place to see how much money Luke should bring to the store to cover the cost of the radio and the sales tax.

Luke should bring ________ dollars to the store.

11.

12.

13.

CHAPTER 2 POSTTEST

NAME ____________________

Check What You Know

Adding and Subtracting 2- and 3-Digit Numbers (with renaming)

Add.

	a	b	c	d	e	f
1.	27 + 43	86 + 92	135 + 47	82 + 13	45 + 154	87 + 196
2.	387 + 405	786 + 193	150 + 270	863 + 42	323 + 46	76 + 84
3.	32 + 196	46 + 231	87 + 121	76 + 93	23 + 54	186 + 231
4.	65 + 15	28 + 93	57 + 761	192 + 775	423 + 176	23 + 45

Subtract.

	a	b	c	d	e	f
5.	123 − 15	87 − 23	545 − 35	79 − 63	187 − 93	782 − 143
6.	898 − 454	763 − 321	981 − 133	725 − 123	805 − 73	120 − 80
7.	76 − 41	87 − 35	72 − 35	153 − 92	763 − 154	876 − 450
8.	879 − 69	87 − 43	100 − 35	730 − 300	765 − 231	845 − 708

NAME ___________________________

Check What You Know

SHOW YOUR WORK

Adding and Subtracting 2- and 3-Digit Numbers (with renaming)

Solve each problem.

9. Kurt has saved 29 dollars to buy a remote control car. The remote control car that he wants to buy costs 43 dollars. How much more money does he need to save?

Are you to add or subtract? __________

He will need to save __________ more dollars.

10. Latisha sold 36 candy bars on Friday and 45 candy bars on Saturday. How many candy bars did she sell in all?

Are you to add or subtract? __________

Latisha sold __________ candy bars in all.

11. Harry had 57 pennies and 16 dimes. How many coins does he have?

Are you to add or subtract? __________

He has __________ coins.

12. Tawna has 253 pennies. Shawn has 146 pennies. How many more pennies does Tawna have than Shawn?

Tawna has __________ more pennies than Shawn.

13. The team sold 453 tickets for the game. There were 249 adult tickets sold. How many children's tickets were sold?

The team sold __________ children's tickets.

9.

10.

11.

12.

13.

NAME ____________________

Lesson 3.1 Adding 2-Digit Numbers

Add the ones. Add the tens.

```
  75          1              1
 +66         75             75   addend
 ---        +66          +  66   addend
            ---          -----
              1            141   sum
     5 + 6 = 11
```

Add.

	a	b	c	d	e	f
1.	23 + 95 = 118	17 + 86	90 + 50	72 + 46	87 + 23	97 + 65
2.	19 + 75	26 + 93	47 + 58	54 + 59	64 + 94	87 + 27
3.	23 + 79	38 + 81	75 + 86	23 + 92	86 + 41	39 + 82
4.	43 + 71	65 + 39	37 + 82	19 + 83	43 + 62	75 + 95
5.	60 + 40	20 + 87	23 + 97	26 + 85	94 + 45	23 + 63
6.	67 + 72	95 + 92	83 + 67	49 + 69	27 + 99	82 + 57

NAME ______________________

Lesson 3.1 Problem Solving

SHOW YOUR WORK

Solve each problem.

1. Sarah earned 58 dollars last week from her paper route. This week she earned 47 dollars. How much money did she earn for both weeks combined?

   She earned __________ dollars last week.

   She earned __________ dollars this week.

   She earned __________ dollars for both weeks combined.

2. Eduardo has 72 dollars in his savings account. How much money will be in his savings account if he deposits 43 dollars today?

   He has __________ dollars.

   He will deposit __________ dollars.

   He will have a total of __________ dollars in his savings account.

3. Flo read a book with 92 pages. Sofia read a book with 87 pages. How many pages did they both read?

   Flo read __________ pages.

   Sofia read __________ pages.

   Together they read __________ pages.

4. At the wedding reception there were 77 adults and 52 children. How many people were at the wedding reception?

   There were __________ adults.

   There were __________ children.

   There were __________ people at the wedding reception.

1.

2.

3.

4.

NAME ___________________________

Lesson 3.2 Subtracting 2 Digits from 3 Digits

	Subtract the ones.	To subtract the tens, rename the 1 hundred and 2 tens as "12 tens."	Subtract the tens.	
125	125	~~1~~ ~~2~~ 5 (12 written above)	~~1~~ ~~2~~ 5 (12 written above)	minuend
− 84	− 84	− 84	− 84	subtrahend
	1	1	41	difference

Subtract.

	a	b	c	d	e	f
1.	173 − 33 = 140	121 − 60	195 − 44	122 − 11	147 − 53	182 − 90
2.	143 − 62	180 − 70	119 − 15	123 − 12	186 − 65	187 − 42
3.	154 − 13	127 − 83	187 − 67	135 − 42	115 − 24	171 − 60
4.	132 − 51	177 − 43	192 − 71	186 − 92	134 − 72	125 − 45
5.	129 − 86	176 − 75	120 − 40	194 − 53	189 − 62	134 − 42
6.	165 − 51	167 − 45	150 − 30	157 − 63	149 − 61	139 − 62
7.	175 − 82	167 − 43	133 − 41	148 − 78	165 − 43	128 − 57

NAME ______________________

Lesson 3.2 Subtracting 2 Digits from 3 Digits

	Rename 5 tens and 3 ones as "4 tens and 13 ones."	Subtract the ones.	Rename 1 hundred and 4 tens as "14 tens."	Subtract the tens.	
153	4 13 1 ~~5~~ ~~3~~	4 13 1 ~~5~~ ~~3~~	14 13 ~~1~~ ~~5~~ ~~3~~	14 13 ~~1~~ ~~5~~ ~~3~~	minuend
− 65	− 65	− 65	− 65	− 65	subtrahend
		8	8	88	difference

Subtract.

	a	b	c	d	e	f
1.	162 − 73 = 89	175 − 97	182 − 94	103 − 17	116 − 39	127 − 88
2.	174 − 95	147 − 68	132 − 65	115 − 49	107 − 39	181 − 95
3.	101 − 75	100 − 92	127 − 79	133 − 44	142 − 73	135 − 47
4.	141 − 63	137 − 79	142 − 73	153 − 67	155 − 96	164 − 88
5.	100 − 72	106 − 48	117 − 88	124 − 66	163 − 89	180 − 93
6.	172 − 87	161 − 92	145 − 66	132 − 57	130 − 43	120 − 62
7.	164 − 85	152 − 63	144 − 87	157 − 69	123 − 45	174 − 87

NAME ____________________

Lesson 3.2 Subtracting 2 Digits from 3 Digits

Subtract.

	a	b	c	d	e	f
1.	132 − 71	196 − 87	165 − 59	163 − 71	119 − 29	107 − 76
2.	106 − 51	100 − 29	153 − 69	147 − 88	192 − 75	173 − 62
3.	175 − 95	169 − 99	142 − 37	140 − 93	131 − 57	123 − 45
4.	167 − 76	173 − 82	192 − 95	143 − 77	126 − 54	119 − 38
5.	117 − 26	100 − 33	175 − 46	142 − 57	136 − 47	121 − 32
6.	176 − 89	143 − 54	140 − 39	173 − 75	163 − 92	159 − 46
7.	144 − 86	122 − 31	191 − 75	175 − 93	144 − 65	136 − 42
8.	121 − 37	106 − 42	165 − 43	162 − 47	181 − 57	169 − 82
9.	106 − 99	127 − 49	136 − 58	124 − 75	143 − 52	182 − 95

NAME ___________________________

Lesson 3.2 Problem Solving

SHOW YOUR WORK

Solve each problem.

1. There are 119 houses on Green Street. The postal carrier has only 57 flyers to deliver to Green Street. How many more flyers does he need?

   The postal carrier needs __________ flyers.

   He has __________ flyers.

   He needs __________ more flyers.

2. There are 162 days of school in a school year. This year, David has gone to school for 54 days. How many more days will David need to go to school?

   There are __________ days of school.

   David has gone to __________ days of school.

   David needs to go to school for __________ more days.

3. Ivanna has 117 pennies. She buys a candy bar for 59 pennies. How many pennies does she have left?

   Ivanna has __________ pennies.

   She spent __________ pennies.

   She has __________ pennies left.

4. There are 153 students in third grade. If 62 students did not go on the field trip to the zoo, how many students did go on the field trip?

   There are __________ students in the third grade.

   __________ students did not go on the field trip.

   __________ students went on the field trip.

1.
2.
3.
4.

NAME ____________________

Lesson 3.3 Adding 3-Digit Numbers

	Add the ones.	Add the tens.	Add the hundreds.
755 + 469	1 755 + 469 = 4	1 1 755 + 469 = 24	1 1 755 + 469 = 1224

Add.

	a	b	c	d	e	f
1.	123 + 562 = 685	982 + 171	342 + 591	782 + 341	123 + 321	681 + 975
2.	862 + 313	900 + 130	720 + 850	931 + 111	823 + 457	547 + 321
3.	861 + 421	862 + 139	431 + 250	782 + 191	751 + 605	871 + 323
4.	791 + 191	144 + 800	192 + 175	257 + 147	203 + 211	541 + 693
5.	705 + 719	641 + 209	873 + 505	700 + 650	105 + 341	450 + 362
6.	593 + 741	861 + 209	735 + 145	820 + 431	738 + 387	719 + 120
7.	153 + 312	712 + 210	619 + 715	205 + 316	153 + 814	613 + 261

NAME ____________________

Lesson 3.3 Problem Solving

SHOW YOUR WORK

Solve each problem.

1. At the basketball game, 232 adult tickets were sold and 179 children's tickets were sold. How many tickets were sold for the basketball game?

There were __________ adult tickets sold.

There were __________ children's tickets sold.

There were __________ total tickets sold.

2. At the local elementary school there are 543 boys and 476 girls. How many total students are there?

There are __________ boys.

There are __________ girls.

There are __________ total students.

3. Mr. Gomez has 639 blue tiles and 722 green tiles. How many blue and green tiles does Mr. Gomez have?

Mr. Gomez has __________ blue tiles.

He has __________ green tiles.

He has __________ blue and green tiles.

4. The shoe store has 324 pairs of athletic shoes and 187 pairs of sandals. How many athletic shoes and sandals does the shoe store have in all?

There are __________ pairs of athletic shoes.

There are __________ pairs of sandals.

There are __________ pairs of athletic shoes and sandals in all.

1.

2.

3.

4.

NAME ____________________

Lesson 3.4 Subtracting 3-Digit Numbers

	Rename 2 tens and 1 one as "1 ten and 11 ones." Then, subtract the ones.	Rename 6 hundreds and 1 ten as "5 hundreds and 11 tens." Then, subtract the tens.	Subtract the hundreds.
621 −259	6~~2~~~~1~~ (1 11) −259 2	~~6~~~~2~~~~1~~ (5 11 11) −259 62	~~6~~~~2~~~~1~~ (5 11 11) minuend −259 subtrahend 362 difference

Subtract.

	a	b	c	d	e	f
1.	321 −109 212	745 −152	639 −150	830 −710	626 −146	457 −309
2.	729 −321	657 −451	386 −107	411 −305	486 −109	311 −121
3.	983 −652	971 −572	876 −357	549 −360	721 −144	958 −637
4.	256 −142	347 −139	725 −196	863 −692	980 −532	720 −500
5.	543 −457	762 −135	132 −107	921 −571	631 −545	982 −144
6.	531 −250	720 −371	582 −357	793 −457	612 −483	592 −107

NAME ____________________

Lesson 3.4 Problem Solving

SHOW YOUR WORK

Solve each problem.

1. There are 990 seats at the stadium. If there are 587 people at the stadium, how many empty seats are there?

   There are ________ stadium seats.

   There are ________ people.

   There are ________ empty seats.

2. A bicycle cost 530 dollars. There is a rebate for 147 dollars. How much will the bike cost after the rebate?

   The bicycle costs ________ dollars.

   The rebate is ________ dollars.

   The cost of the bicycle after the rebate is ________ dollars.

3. There were 600 green and yellow paper clips in the package. If 230 were green, how many were yellow?

   There were a total of ________ paper clips.

   There were ________ green paper clips.

   There were ________ yellow paper clips.

4. The ice cream store sold 349 scoops of ice cream on Monday. The store sold 178 scoops of ice cream on Tuesday. How many more scoops did the store sell on Monday?

   The ice cream store sold ________ more scoops on Monday than on Tuesday.

5. Last year, Randy received a set of 360 toy cars. This year, Randy counted only 163 toy cars in his set. How many toy cars had Randy lost?

   Randy lost ________ toy cars.

1.

2.

3.

4.

5.

NAME ____________________

Lesson 3.5 Thinking Subtraction for Addition

To check
215 + 109 = 324,
subtract 109 from 324.

```
  215  <---┐
+ 109      |
-----      |
  324      These should be the same.
- 109      |
-----      |
  215  <---┘
```

Add. Check each answer.

	a	b	c	d	e	f
1.	157 + 212 = 369; check: 369 − 212 = 157	719 + 182	312 + 105	213 + 519	306 + 215	120 + 170
2.	710 + 398	357 + 249	712 + 363	714 + 291	312 + 85	419 + 57
3.	300 + 547	591 + 120	612 + 319	425 + 125	411 + 120	247 + 259
4.	863 + 192	459 + 130	603 + 209	711 + 191	252 + 130	412 + 283

NAME ______________________

Lesson 3.6 Thinking Addition for Subtraction

To check

982 – 657 = 325,

add 657 to 325.

```
  982  <---┐
 −657      |
 ----      |
  325      These should be the same.
 +657      |
 ----      |
  982  <---┘
```

Subtract. Check each answer.

	a	b	c	d	e	f
1.	720 − 150 = 570 570 + 150 = 720	321 − 83	125 − 92	983 − 657	456 − 291	442 − 220
2.	300 − 179	119 − 104	423 − 197	259 − 147	592 − 463	708 − 412
3.	519 − 120	540 − 320	192 − 86	710 − 447	683 − 419	712 − 307
4.	719 − 532	919 − 457	687 − 250	912 − 609	542 − 327	728 − 530

NAME ______________________

Lesson 3.7 Addition and Subtraction Practice

Add or subtract.

	a	b	c	d	e	f
1.	39 + 92	86 + 93	132 − 41	186 − 92	543 − 121	125 + 89
2.	76 + 192	154 − 92	543 − 206	150 − 90	650 + 129	920 − 860
3.	137 + 310	159 − 82	185 − 96	432 − 257	710 − 512	819 − 720
4.	541 + 862	432 − 119	720 + 140	186 − 107	540 − 75	413 + 356
5.	812 + 93	712 − 347	690 − 320	451 − 253	512 − 308	803 + 112
6.	119 + 104	703 + 219	861 − 172	186 + 210	513 − 211	179 − 86
7.	120 − 45	198 − 79	312 − 192	519 + 130	710 + 195	712 − 419
8.	412 − 306	790 − 205	157 + 192	175 − 84	192 + 210	786 − 442
9.	510 + 834	674 − 556	700 − 310	120 + 460	690 − 541	710 − 82

NAME ______________________

Lesson 3.8 Addition and Subtraction Practice

Add or subtract.

	a	b	c	d	e	f
1.	72 +59	76 +82	138 − 52	192 − 75	310 +354	763 −123
2.	191 +210	583 −421	710 −190	54 +86	93 +104	210 −108
3.	582 +529	711 −547	712 − 92	860 +139	786 −457	259 +457
4.	186 +211	210 −102	96 +87	310 + 99	386 +503	710 −605
5.	232 −144	457 −310	386 +205	740 −310	862 −456	415 −209
6.	392 − 86	510 − 47	610 −232	192 − 86	191 +212	138 +493
7.	205 +472	437 +291	186 +396	408 +520	393 −121	683 −541
8.	386 −130	149 +310	186 − 93	110 +342	186 − 90	310 +620
9.	130 +210	190 − 70	163 +292	145 + 96	192 + 47	186 + 57

NAME ____________________

Check What You Learned

Adding and Subtracting 2- and 3-Digit Numbers (with renaming)

Add.

	a	b	c	d	e	f
1.	75 +92	135 +210	193 + 56	310 + 92	513 +409	746 +122
2.	193 + 86	183 +192	842 +908	109 +236	963 +310	150 +210
3.	512 +457	310 + 97	510 +346	910 +132	512 +403	912 + 78
4.	543 +286	123 +592	647 +382	442 + 85	123 210 +392	212 391 +407

Subtract.

	a	b	c	d	e	f
5.	172 − 35	192 − 86	174 − 96	120 − 80	310 − 40	293 −107
6.	986 −698	862 −245	352 −121	187 − 72	647 −253	547 −183
7.	662 −503	708 −231	456 −269	882 −199	753 −268	712 −543
8.	712 −402	548 −213	593 −369	610 −132	782 −441	192 − 85

CHAPTER 3 POSTTEST

NAME ____________________

Check What You Learned

SHOW YOUR WORK

Adding and Subtracting 2- and 3-Digit Numbers (with renaming)

Solve each problem.

9. For a game of checkers, 24 checkers are needed. There are only 18 checkers in the box. How many checkers are missing?

There are ________ checkers missing.

10. An adult has 32 teeth. A child has 24 teeth. How many more teeth does the adult have?

An adult has ________ more teeth than a child.

11. Sam weighed 232 pounds. He lost 13 pounds. How much does Sam weigh now?

Sam weighs ________ pounds.

12. Alvin has 532 pennies. Regina has 691 pennies. How many pennies do they have together?

Alvin and Regina have ________ pennies together.

13. Mr. Ito is 53 years old. His daughter, Kimi, is 25. How much older is Mr. Ito than his daughter?

Mr. Ito is ________ years older than his daughter.

14. Mr. and Mrs. Acosta have been married for 47 years. Mrs. Acosta was 29 when she married Mr. Acosta. How old is Mrs. Acosta now?

Mrs. Acosta is ________ years old.

9.

10.

11.

12.

13.

14.

NAME ____________________

Check What You Know

Adding and Subtracting to 4 Digits (with renaming)

Add or subtract.

	a	b	c	d	e
1.	13 7 +19	23 42 +97	22 24 +16	8 9 +5	21 47 +58
2.	123 415 +423	190 180 +360	420 567 +321	519 612 +313	423 521 +747
3.	1436 +5120	5190 +4125	5032 +1764	4321 +2841	5960 +4011
4.	3121 +1076	1300 +2900	4320 +1051	1905 +1706	5190 +3049
5.	1340 − 380	1960 − 420	720 −340	5120 −1780	4963 −1082
6.	5947 −4272	5803 −1992	1906 −1173	1876 − 759	4120 −3290
7.	9645 −6823	312 − 20	421 − 30	1500 −1200	4500 − 720
8.	860 −729	9120 −7210	8160 −2400	4242 − 963	4163 −3552

NAME ____________________

Check What You Know

SHOW YOUR WORK

Adding and Subtracting to 4 Digits (with renaming)

Solve each problem.

9. Gerod has 5 birds, 3 turtles, 2 hamsters, and 1 dog. How many pets does he have?

   Gerod has __________ pets.

10. Oleta has 19 dimes, 27 quarters, 153 pennies, and 6 nickels. How many coins does she have?

    Oleta has __________ coins.

11. James received 100 dollars for his birthday. He spent 63 dollars of it on two computer games. How much money does he have left?

    James has __________ dollars left.

12. At a basketball game, one team scored 36 points. The other team scored 27 points. How many total points were scored in the game?

    There were a total of __________ points scored in the basketball game.

13. In the year 1998, an antique vase was 239 years old. In what year was the vase made?

    The vase was made in the year __________.

14. During his walk each day, Paul counted his steps. In 4 days, he walked 420, 980, 642, and 760 steps. How many steps did he walk?

    Paul walked __________ steps in 4 days.

9.

10.

11.

12.

13.

14.

NAME ____________________

Lesson 4.1 Adding 3 or More Numbers (1- and 2-digit)

Add the ones. Add the tens.

45	5		1	1
62	2	7	45	45
+94	+4	+ 4	62	62
		11 or 10 + 1	+94	+ 94
			1	201

Add.

	a	b	c	d	e	f
1.	3 6 +9 18	7 5 +8	6 12 +13	8 17 +19	12 32 +53	8 6 +2
2.	17 93 +23	16 45 +92	82 18 +23	7 19 +57	22 86 +34	50 40 +60
3.	86 93 +72	23 35 +62	18 35 +67	86 54 +83	32 49 +76	13 19 +23
4.	25 66 +72	81 19 +83	53 42 +93	13 12 +14	10 20 +90	82 76 +54
5.	86 54 32 +52	92 10 53 +47	81 71 36 +27	12 18 24 +19	93 48 13 +27	41 86 53 +22

NAME ____________________

Lesson 4.1 Problem Solving

SHOW YOUR WORK

Solve each problem.

1. The bubble gum dispenser has 23 blue gumballs, 16 red gumballs, 14 yellow gumballs, and 7 green gumballs. How many gumballs are in the dispenser?

   There are ________ blue gumballs.

   There are ________ red gumballs.

   There are ________ yellow gumballs.

   There are ________ green gumballs.

   There are ________ gumballs in the dispenser.

2. In the fruit basket there are 9 apples, 6 bananas, and 7 oranges. How many pieces of fruit are in the fruit basket?

   There are ________ apples.

   There are ________ bananas.

   There are ________ oranges.

   There are ________ pieces of fruit in the basket.

3. Mr. Williams is 53 years old. Mrs. Williams is 44 years old. Their son is 18 years old. What is the combined total of the ages of the Williams family?

   Mr. Williams is ________ years old.

   Mrs. Williams is ________ years old.

   Their son is ________ years old.

   The total of their ages is ________ years.

4. When Hailey went shopping for school supplies, she bought a calculator for 14 dollars, a package of paper for 5 dollars, a calendar for 3 dollars, and a package of pens for 3 dollars. How much did Hailey spend on school supplies?

   Hailey spent ________ dollars on school supplies.

1.

2.

3.

4.

NAME ____________________

Lesson 4.2 Adding 3 or More Numbers (3-digit)

	Add the ones.	Add the tens.	Add the hundreds.
231 457 +625	1 231 457 +625 3	1 1 231 457 +625 13	1 1 231 457 + 625 1313

Add.

	a	b	c	d	e	f
1.	522 367 +151 1040	868 321 +405	150 200 +300	701 231 +862	986 105 +525	129 318 +467
2.	803 623 +186	545 309 +119	868 740 +809	132 195 +118	200 300 +600	180 240 +303
3.	861 757 +409	863 404 +891	731 356 +402	865 591 +217	238 405 +596	898 777 +192
4.	341 127 +192	864 425 +323	127 291 +867	205 876 +198	712 490 +600	750 400 +203
5.	591 603 907 +432	862 191 183 +251	892 645 320 +123	132 169 119 +105	323 309 452 +690	712 613 518 +437

NAME ________________

Lesson 4.2 Problem Solving

SHOW YOUR WORK

Solve each problem.

1. Joe earned 135 dollars during his first week of work. He earned 213 dollars during his second week of work. He earned 159 dollars during his third week of work. How much money did Joe earn during the three weeks that he worked?

   Joe earned _____ dollars during his first week.

   Joe earned _____ dollars during his second week.

   Joe earned _____ dollars during his third week.

   Joe earned _____ dollars for all 3 weeks of work.

2. On the first floor of a 3-story apartment building, there are 186 apartments occupied. On the second floor, there are 175 apartments occupied. On the third floor, there are 182 apartments occupied. How many apartments are occupied in all?

   There are _____ apartments occupied on the first floor.

   There are _____ apartments occupied on the second floor.

   There are _____ apartments occupied on the third floor.

   There are _____ apartments occupied in all.

3. The following numbers of students attend four different schools: 543, 692, 487, and 603. How many students attend all four schools?

   _________ students attend all four schools.

4. In a book, chapter 1 has 112 pages and chapter 2 has 119 pages. Chapter 3 has 103 pages and chapter 4 has 108 pages. How many pages are in the book?

   There are _____ pages in the book.

1.	
2.	
3.	4.

NAME ______________________

Lesson 4.3 Adding 4-Digit Numbers

	Add the ones.	Add the tens.	Add the hundreds.	Add the thousands.
3746	3746	3746	3746	3746
+5899	+5899	+5899	+5899	+5899
	5	45	645	9645

Add.

	a	b	c	d	e	f
1.	7865 +1192 9057	8654 +1219	4320 +3069	3543 +3921	4293 +5176	6405 +3398
2.	1982 +1782	7083 +2907	4325 +4986	6057 +1239	8761 +1032	2305 +5747
3.	3050 +4707	6932 +2349	5437 +2968	1718 +2347	7923 +1250	4523 +3962
4.	5431 +2989	7986 +1479	1119 +2459	7239 +1635	2450 +7267	6527 +2985
5.	5431 +1982	7986 +1246	1543 +3989	7121 +1923	8763 +1005	4321 +2387
6.	5450 +1987	4733 +2576	3981 +2877	6986 +2928	7181 +2111	7900 +2005

NAME ___________________________

Lesson 4.3 Problem Solving

SHOW YOUR WORK

Solve each problem.

1. Two local high schools have 1,523 students and 1,695 students. How many students are there at both high schools together?

One high school has __________ students.

The other high school has __________students.

There are a total of __________ students at both high schools.

1.

2. Monica started at an elevation of 1,200 feet for her hiking trip. She hiked up the mountain for 1,320 feet in elevation. How high did she hike?

Monica started at __________ feet in elevation.

She hiked __________ feet in elevation.

She hiked up to an elevation of __________ feet.

2.

3. Steve has a coin worth 1,050 dollars. He has another coin worth 1,072 dollars. How much are both coins worth?

Both coins are worth __________ dollars.

3.

4. Roy ran 1,100 yards as a running back during his junior year of high school. During his senior year of high school, he ran 1,500 yards as a running back. How many yards did he run in both years combined?

Roy ran a total of __________ yards for both his junior and senior year of high school.

4.

NAME ______________________

Lesson 4.4 Subtracting to 4 Digits

	Subtract the ones.	Rename 4 hundreds and 3 tens as "3 hundreds and 13 tens." Subtract the tens.	Rename 5 thousands and 3 hundreds as "4 thousands and 13 hundreds." Subtract the hundreds.	Subtract the thousands.
5437 − 1592	5437 − 1592 5	5 $\overset{3}{\not4}$ $\overset{13}{\not3}$ 7 − 1592 45	$\overset{4}{\not5}$ $\overset{13}{\not4}$ $\overset{13}{\not3}$ 7 − 1592 845	$\overset{4}{\not5}$ $\overset{13}{\not4}$ $\overset{13}{\not3}$ 7 − 1592 3845

Subtract.

	a	b	c	d	e
1.	9865 − 2382 7483	7528 − 792	8654 − 3993	1925 − 183	1876 − 982
2.	5473 − 3591	8762 − 682	7945 − 963	8654 − 772	7846 − 3974
3.	6932 − 2840	1389 − 794	2545 − 963	7863 − 2572	8121 − 640
4.	7865 − 974	3456 − 661	7982 − 490	8163 − 4670	4325 − 1534
5.	9876 − 985	8716 − 5823	5432 − 3651	3287 − 395	7805 − 164
6.	5439 − 767	4321 − 841	7865 − 974	7976 − 4682	5439 − 866

NAME ___________________________

Lesson 4.4 Problem Solving

SHOW YOUR WORK

Solve each problem.

1. There are 2,532 students at the school. 1,341 are girls. How many are boys?

There are __________ students.

There are __________ girls.

There are __________ boys.

2. In 2003, the average rent for a house was 1,250 dollars per month. In 1944, the average rent for a house was 495 dollars per month. How much higher was the rent in 2003 than in 1944?

Rent in 2003 was __________ dollars per month.

Rent in 1944 was __________ dollars per month.

Rent in 2003 was __________ dollars per month higher than in 1944.

3. In the year 1986, Mrs. Olveras turned 103 years old. In what year was she born?

In the year __________,

Mrs. Olveras turned __________ years old.

Mrs. Olveras was born in __________.

4. In the year 1996, Mr. Smith's car was considered a classic. The car was made in 1942. How old is Mr. Smith's car?

Mr. Smith's car is __________ years old.

5. Kayla wants to visit her grandmother who lives 2,583 miles away. The airplane will only take her 2,392 miles toward her destination. Kayla needs to rent a car to drive the remaining miles. How many miles does Kayla need to drive?

Kayla would need to drive __________ miles.

1.	
2.	
3.	
4.	5.

NAME ____________________

Lesson 4.5 Estimating Addition

Round each number to the highest place value the numbers have in common. Then, add from right to left.

194 → 190		203 → 200	
+ 76 → + 80		+196 → +200	
270		400	

The highest place value for 194 and 76 is the tens place. Round 194 and 76 to the tens place. Add.

The highest place value for 203 and 196 is the hundreds place. Round 203 and 196 to the hundreds place. Add.

Estimate each sum.

	a		b	c	d
1.	25 + 36	30 + 40 = 70	23 + 14	57 + 51	42 + 92
2.	92 + 51		131 + 42	165 + 92	147 + 97
3.	147 + 362	100 + 400 = 500	175 + 302	457 + 603	543 + 261
4.	1132 + 432		1250 + 347	5786 + 432	4679 + 578
5.	1562 + 3492	2000 + 3000 = 5000	6054 + 6542	3541 + 7987	2795 + 2454

NAME ____________________

Lesson 4.5 Problem Solving

SHOW YOUR WORK

Solve each problem by using estimation.

1. Kirima read 534 pages last week and 352 pages this week. About how many pages did Kirima read?

   Kirima read about __________ pages.

2. Tim has 13 dollars. James has 15 dollars. About how many dollars do they have together?

   Tim and James have about __________ dollars together.

3. Mr. Hwan had 532 dollars in his savings account before he made a deposit of 259 dollars. About how much money does he have in his savings account now?

   Mr. Hwan has about __________ dollars in his savings account now.

4. Mrs. Luna is 43 years old. Mrs. Turner is 52 years old. Mrs. Rockwell is 39 years old. About how much is their combined age?

   Their combined age is about __________ years.

5. Marla bought 4 boards at the home center. The boards were 86, 103, 152, and 161 inches long. About how many inches of boards did Marla buy?

   Marla bought about __________ inches of boards.

1.

2.

3.

4.

5.

NAME ______________________

Lesson 4.6 Estimating Subtraction

Round each number to the highest place value the numbers have in common. Then, subtract from right to left.

236 →	240		396 →	400	
− 49 →	− 50		−287 →	−300	
	190			100	

The highest place value for 236 and 49 is the tens place. Round 236 and 49 to the tens place. Subtract.

The highest place value for 396 and 287 is the hundreds place. Round 396 and 287 to the hundreds place. Subtract.

Estimate each difference.

	a		b	c	d
1.	56 − 43	60 − 40 = 20	49 − 12	72 − 61	80 − 45
2.	451 − 72		986 − 59	760 − 32	542 − 57
3.	543 − 290	500 − 300 = 200	943 − 457	547 − 249	686 − 162
4.	1543 − 661		3247 − 843	4560 − 493	7631 − 647
5.	8798 − 4453	9000 − 4000 = 5000	9476 − 2652	7345 − 6443	9432 − 1486

NAME ______________________

Lesson 4.6 Problem Solving

SHOW YOUR WORK

Solve each problem by using estimation.

1. Fred had 39 dollars. He gave 23 dollars to Kim. About how much money does Fred have left?

   Fred has about __________ dollars left.

2. There are 186 apartments in an apartment building. 92 are not rented. About how many apartments are rented?

   There are about __________ rented apartments.

3. Sue wants to buy a bicycle for 560 dollars. She has 430 dollars. About how much more money does she need to buy the bicycle?

   Sue needs about __________ more dollars to buy the bicycle.

4. At the theater, 98 adult tickets were sold. If 210 tickets were sold, about how many children's tickets were sold?

   About __________ children's tickets were sold.

5. Kelly bought a roll of cloth 197 inches long. She cut 85 inches off the roll to use in a project. About how many inches did she have left on the roll?

   Kelly had about __________ inches left on the roll.

1.

2.

3.

4.

5.

NAME ____________________

Check What You Learned

Adding and Subtracting to 4 Digits (with renaming)

Add or subtract.

	a	b	c	d	e
1.	23 13 +27	8 36 +45	72 38 +43	20 35 +47	86 93 +10
2.	123 427 +192	86 425 +119	19 87 +425	295 221 +196	425 196 176 +105
3.	4321 +1972	5916 + 432	8764 + 492	4567 +1986	5921 +2053
4.	4321 +1985	4321 + 986	4986 +2045	3096 +1779	4305 + 300
5.	3865 − 974	4321 −2280	9871 −4791	4325 −2554	7964 −2872
6.	8212 −6421	9870 −5380	7653 − 482	4987 − 793	1054 − 662
7.	7298 − 792	9784 −6592	4837 −1955	4954 −2063	3219 −1335
8.	8164 −4273	7918 −3633	4327 − 940	9141 −7051	8642 − 951

NAME ___________

Check What You Learned

SHOW YOUR WORK

Adding and Subtracting to 4 Digits (with renaming)

Solve each problem.

9. Jerry has 37 red marbles, 42 blue marbles, 13 black marbles, and 23 yellow marbles. How many marbles does Jerry have?

Jerry has ___________ marbles.

9.

10. In the year 1976, Mrs. Lopez was 82 years old. In what year was she born?

Mrs. Lopez was born in ___________.

10.

11. Estella is 23 years old, Lydia is 27 years old, Toni is 42 years old, and Mai is 18 years old. What are their combined ages?

Their combined ages equal ___________ years.

11.

12. Marty earned 586 dollars one week at his job and 432 dollars the next week. Estimate about how much money Marty earned for both weeks.

Marty earned about ___________ dollars for both weeks.

12.

13. Holly needs to make 72 cookies for the school bake sale. She has already made 37 cookies. Estimate about how many more cookies she needs to make.

Holly needs to make about ___________ more cookies.

13.

NAME ____________________

Check What You Know

Multiplying through 2 Digits by 1 Digit

CHAPTER 5 PRETEST

Multiply.

	a	b	c	d	e	f
1.	2×0	5×1	4×3	0×2	5×6	3×8
2.	7×2	9×3	8×8	6×3	4×5	5×4
3.	6×6	3×9	1×7	5×3	2×6	2×2
4.	3×0	4×7	6×9	4×4	5×1	2×9
5.	7×4	3×7	2×3	4×2	9×1	6×5
6.	20×4	14×3	29×3	32×4	96×2	81×1
7.	46×4	72×1	61×3	70×2	52×4	13×5
8.	21×5	15×3	31×4	90×2	56×3	43×3
9.	18×3	22×4	31×2	54×5	59×1	15×4

NAME ____________________

Check What You Know

SHOW YOUR WORK

Multiplying through 2 Digits by 1 Digit

Solve each problem.

10. John bought four 23-cent stamps. How many cents did John spend on stamps?

The stamps cost __________ cents.

11. A clown had 13 balloons that he sold at a carnival for 5 cents each. If he sold all 13 balloons, how much money did he make?

The clown made __________ cents.

12. The movie rental store charges 3 dollars to rent each movie. Miss Padilla rents 5 movies. How much will the movie rental store charge her?

The movie rental store will charge Miss Padilla

__________ dollars.

13. Each semester Henry takes 5 classes. After 8 semesters, how many classes did Henry take?

Henry took __________ classes.

14. Sally wants to buy 3 stickers. The stickers each cost 25 cents. How much will Sally spend on the 3 stickers?

Sally will spend __________ cents on the 3 stickers.

10.
11.
12.
13.
14.

NAME ______________________

Lesson 5.1 Understanding Multiplication

two times seven
2 × 7 means 7 + 7

$$\begin{array}{rl} 7 & \text{factor} \\ \times\ 2 & \text{factor} \\ \hline 14 & \text{product} \end{array} \qquad \begin{array}{r} 7 \\ +\ 7 \\ \hline 14 \end{array}$$

five times three
5 × 3 means 5 + 5 + 5

$$\begin{array}{rl} 5 & \text{factor} \\ \times\ 3 & \text{factor} \\ \hline 15 & \text{product} \end{array} \qquad \begin{array}{r} 5 \\ 5 \\ +\ 5 \\ \hline 15 \end{array}$$

Multiply. Write the corresponding addition problem next to each multiplication problem.

	a	b	c	d	e
1.	3 × 2 = 6 (3 + 3 = 6)	7 × 2	6 × 2	9 × 2	8 × 2
2.	2 × 2	1 × 2	5 × 3	6 × 3	3 × 3
3.	2 × 3	1 × 3	4 × 3	7 × 3	2 × 4
4.	4 × 4	1 × 4	5 × 4	9 × 4	8 × 4
5.	3 × 4	4 × 2	5 × 2	8 × 3	9 × 3
6.	6 × 4	7 × 4	3 × 2	7 × 3	9 × 2

Lesson 5.2 Multiplying through 5 × 9

factor 3 → Find the **3**-row.
factor × 7 → Find the **7**-column.
product 21 ← The product is named where the 3-row and the 7-column meet.

7-column

3-row

x	0	1	2	3	4	5	6	7	8	9
0	0	0	0	0	0	0	0	0	0	0
1	0	1	2	3	4	5	6	7	8	9
2	0	2	4	6	8	10	12	14	16	18
3	0	3	6	9	12	15	18	21	24	27
4	0	4	8	12	16	20	24	28	32	36
5	0	5	10	15	20	25	30	35	40	45
6	0	6	12	18	24	30				
7	0	7	14	21	28	35				
8	0	8	16	24	32	40				
9	0	9	18	27	36	45				

Multiply.

	a	b	c	d	e	f
1.	5 × 0 = 0	3 × 9	6 × 5	1 × 4	5 × 1	6 × 3
2.	9 × 2	8 × 5	5 × 8	0 × 0	2 × 9	3 × 4
3.	4 × 6	7 × 3	6 × 1	7 × 2	3 × 5	4 × 1
4.	6 × 2	5 × 5	9 × 1	2 × 4	3 × 7	7 × 0
5.	0 × 9	3 × 6	7 × 5	5 × 6	3 × 2	4 × 2
6.	7 × 4	3 × 3	1 × 9	2 × 7	0 × 6	1 × 3

NAME ______________________________

Lesson 5.3 Multiplying through 9 × 9

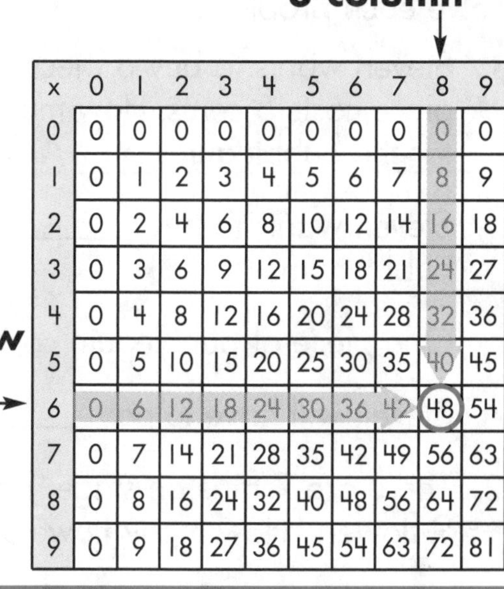

x	0	1	2	3	4	5	6	7	8	9
0	0	0	0	0	0	0	0	0	0	0
1	0	1	2	3	4	5	6	7	8	9
2	0	2	4	6	8	10	12	14	16	18
3	0	3	6	9	12	15	18	21	24	27
4	0	4	8	12	16	20	24	28	32	36
5	0	5	10	15	20	25	30	35	40	45
6	0	6	12	18	24	30	36	42	48	54
7	0	7	14	21	28	35	42	49	56	63
8	0	8	16	24	32	40	48	56	64	72
9	0	9	18	27	36	45	54	63	72	81

factor 6 → Find the **6**-row.
factor × 8 → Find the **8**-column.
product 48 ← The product is named where the 6-row and the 8-column meet.

Multiply.

	a	b	c	d	e	f
1.	3 × 9 = 27	7 × 6	5 × 4	7 × 9	8 × 6	5 × 0
2.	4 × 3	8 × 5	4 × 9	3 × 0	5 × 7	2 × 9
3.	5 × 1	4 × 6	8 × 2	6 × 8	4 × 0	0 × 9
4.	3 × 1	6 × 4	9 × 2	3 × 4	6 × 3	5 × 6
5.	3 × 8	3 × 6	7 × 6	9 × 9	8 × 4	5 × 3
6.	2 × 6	8 × 8	9 × 3	7 × 4	8 × 0	7 × 7

NAME ____________________

Lesson 5.3 Problem Solving

SHOW YOUR WORK

Solve each problem.

1. Steven wants to buy 6 pieces of bubblegum. Each piece costs 5 cents. How much will he have to pay for the bubblegum?

Steven wants to buy __________ pieces of bubblegum.

One piece of bubblegum costs __________ cents.

Steven will have to pay __________ cents total.

2. There are 7 girls on stage. Each girl is holding 9 flowers. How many flowers are there in all?

There are __________ girls.

Each girl is holding __________ flowers.

There are __________ flowers in all.

3. There are 4 rows of desks. There are 8 desks in each row. How many desks are there in all?

There are __________ rows of desks.

There are __________ desks in each row.

There are __________ desks in all.

4. Sara earns 4 dollars a day babysitting her cousin. If Sara babysits for 5 days, how much money will she earn?

Sara will earn __________ dollars.

5. Jose made 4 points in each of the basketball game's 4 quarters. How many points did he make by the end of the game?

He made a total of __________ points.

1.

2.

3.

4.

5.

NAME ____________________

Lesson 5.4 Multiplying 2 Digits by 1 Digit

	Multiply 2 ones by 3.	Multiply 8 tens by 3.		
82	82	82	82	← factor
× 3	× 3	× 3	× 3	← factor
	6	6	6	Add.
		240	+240	
			246	product

Multiply.

	a	b	c	d	e	f
1.	73 × 2 = 6 + 140 = 146	14 × 2	90 × 5	45 × 1	33 × 3	62 × 3
2.	22 × 4	86 × 1	52 × 4	31 × 5	46 × 1	32 × 4
3.	19 × 1	21 × 4	43 × 3	27 × 1	91 × 5	83 × 2
4.	56 × 1	52 × 2	63 × 3	73 × 1	62 × 2	35 × 1

NAME ______________________

Lesson 5.4 Multiplication Practice

	Multiply 2 ones by 4.	Multiply 7 tens by 4.
$\begin{array}{r} 72 \\ \times\ 4 \\ \hline \end{array}$	$\begin{array}{r} 72 \\ \times\ 4 \\ \hline 8 \end{array}$	$\begin{array}{r} 72 \\ \times\ 4 \\ \hline 288 \end{array}$

Multiply.

	a	b	c	d	e	f
1.	31×5	42×2	36×1	52×4	83×3	75×1
2.	39×1	41×4	52×2	28×1	13×3	30×5
3.	54×2	17×1	29×0	23×3	42×4	41×5
4.	61×5	72×3	14×2	86×1	47×1	92×3
5.	83×2	42×3	69×3	11×5	61×2	58×1
6.	13×2	10×5	23×2	42×1	82×4	31×4
7.	22×3	33×2	43×3	52×3	92×2	54×1

NAME ______________________

Lesson 5.5 Multiply 2 Digits by 1 Digit (with renaming)

Multiply 6 ones by 3.

Multiply 2 tens by 3. Add the 1 ten.

26	26 (carry 1)		26 (carry 1)	26 ← factor
× 3	× 3		× 3	× 3 ← factor
	8	$3 \times 20 = 60$	78	78 ← product

$3 \times 6 = 18 = 10 + 8$

$60 + 10 = 70$

Multiply.

	a	b	c	d	e	f
1.	37 × 2 = 74	19 × 5	45 × 2	38 × 2	25 × 3	12 × 5
2.	14 × 4	47 × 2	28 × 3	13 × 4	23 × 4	24 × 4
3.	26 × 2	36 × 2	13 × 5	15 × 3	27 × 2	18 × 5
4.	15 × 5	17 × 3	24 × 3	39 × 2	14 × 5	16 × 2
5.	27 × 3	15 × 4	29 × 2	26 × 3	36 × 2	17 × 5
6.	35 × 2	25 × 2	28 × 2	14 × 3	17 × 4	29 × 3

NAME ______________________

Lesson 5.5 Multiplying 2 Digits by 1 Digit (with renaming)

Multiply 9 ones by 5.

Multiply 6 tens by 5. Add the 4 tens.

$$\begin{array}{r} 69 \\ \times\ 5 \\ \hline \end{array}$$

$$\begin{array}{r} {}^{4} \\ 69 \\ \times\ 5 \\ \hline 5 \end{array}$$

$5 \times 9 = 45 = 40 + 5$

$5 \times 60 = 300$

$$\begin{array}{r} {}^{4} \\ 69 \\ \times\ 5 \\ \hline 345 \end{array}$$

69 ← factor
5 ← factor
345 ← product

$300 + 40 = 340 = 300 + 40$

Multiply.

	a	b	c	d	e	f
1.	72 × 5 = 360	38 × 4	29 × 5	27 × 4	25 × 5	36 × 4
2.	54 × 3	96 × 3	84 × 4	92 × 5	47 × 3	86 × 2
3.	45 × 3	23 × 5	86 × 3	73 × 5	22 × 5	56 × 4
4.	64 × 3	93 × 4	86 × 5	43 × 4	38 × 3	74 × 4
5.	34 × 3	28 × 5	37 × 3	46 × 4	23 × 5	83 × 4
6.	44 × 3	59 × 3	82 × 5	74 × 5	63 × 4	47 × 4

NAME ___________________

Lesson 5.6 Multiplication Practice

Multiply.

	a	b	c	d	e	f
1.	13×5	7×2	10×0	81×4	42×2	13×4
2.	52×3	76×5	41×5	3×2	14×3	17×5
3.	45×5	93×3	42×3	33×2	10×5	4×8
4.	51×2	91×1	17×5	31×2	25×5	30×4
5.	32×5	8×7	5×9	4×0	38×1	72×4
6.	6×9	4×7	22×1	19×3	83×2	54×5
7.	6×5	53×3	18×4	8×6	13×2	17×4
8.	7×4	5×0	3×2	8×2	56×2	19×3
9.	46×3	43×3	27×2	18×5	5×4	13×3

NAME ______________________

Lesson 5.6 Problem Solving

SHOW YOUR WORK

Solve each problem.

1. Gary read 3 books with 56 pages each. How many pages did he read in all?

   There are ________ pages in each book.

   Gary read ________ books.

   Gary read ________ pages in all.

2. There are 5 classes at a school. Each class has 32 students. How many students are at the school?

   There are ________ students in each class.

   There are ________ classes.

   There are ________ students in the school.

3. Yolanda used up 4 rolls of film. If each roll has 24 pictures, how many pictures did she take in all?

   Each roll has ________ pictures.

   Yolanda used ________ rolls of film.

   Yolanda took a total of ________ pictures.

4. During a football game, 2 teams play against each other. There are 11 football players on the field for each team. How many football players are on the field during a football game?

   There are ________ football players on the field.

5. There are 12 eggs in a carton of eggs. If Mary buys 6 egg cartons, how many eggs does she have?

   Mary has ________ eggs.

1.

2.

3.

4.

5.

NAME ______________________________

Check What You Learned

Multiplying through 2 Digits by 1 Digit

Multiply.

	a	b	c	d	e	f
1.	1×5	9×9	3×2	5×4	6×3	8×0
2.	9×7	5×2	6×1	8×2	5×7	3×4
3.	6×5	8×3	4×3	0×8	6×2	4×7
4.	13×2	23×4	17×5	42×1	18×0	23×0
5.	54×2	96×2	53×3	33×2	11×5	40×3
6.	71×2	18×3	20×5	14×3	27×1	19×2
7.	29×3	54×5	21×4	23×4	13×5	12×3
8.	20×4	93×2	17×4	15×3	31×3	21×3
9.	22×3	42×3	11×4	32×5	18×5	95×5

CHAPTER 5 POSTTEST

NAME ______________________

Check What You Learned

SHOW YOUR WORK

Multiplying through 2 Digits by 1 Digit

Solve each problem.

10. Kiri has 5 friends. She gave each friend 3 apples. How many apples did Kiri have?

Kiri had __________ apples.

10.

11. Each of Mr. Black's 4 daughters needs new shoes. Each pair of shoes will cost 29 dollars. How much money will Mr. Black spend on all 4 pairs of shoes?

Mr. Black will spend __________ dollars on the 4 pairs of shoes.

11.

12. There are 30 students in each classroom. If there are 5 classrooms, how many total students are there?

There are a total of __________ students.

12.

13. There are 7 friends that each have 2 dollars. How much money do the 7 friends have?

The friends have a total of __________ dollars.

13.

14. There is a total of 33 students in Ms. Walker's class. If each student receives 4 papers, how many papers are there?

There are __________ papers in all.

14.

NAME ______________________

Check What You Know

Division Facts through 81 ÷ 9

CHAPTER 6 PRETEST

Divide.

	a	b	c	d	e
1.	$4\overline{)36}$	$6\overline{)54}$	$4\overline{)8}$	$8\overline{)16}$	$2\overline{)12}$
2.	$6\overline{)18}$	$9\overline{)81}$	$4\overline{)4}$	$6\overline{)30}$	$3\overline{)9}$
3.	$7\overline{)14}$	$3\overline{)21}$	$5\overline{)40}$	$3\overline{)24}$	$4\overline{)16}$
4.	$1\overline{)5}$	$3\overline{)6}$	$5\overline{)10}$	$4\overline{)12}$	$5\overline{)30}$
5.	$7\overline{)49}$	$9\overline{)63}$	$4\overline{)32}$	$2\overline{)14}$	$1\overline{)8}$
6.	$5\overline{)20}$	$1\overline{)8}$	$7\overline{)7}$	$3\overline{)27}$	$5\overline{)35}$
7.	$8\overline{)40}$	$7\overline{)21}$	$9\overline{)45}$	$7\overline{)42}$	$8\overline{)64}$
8.	$2\overline{)18}$	$3\overline{)15}$	$6\overline{)12}$	$6\overline{)24}$	$8\overline{)48}$
9.	$6\overline{)6}$	$2\overline{)8}$	$9\overline{)36}$	$4\overline{)20}$	$2\overline{)16}$

NAME ____________________

Check What You Know

Division Facts through 81 ÷ 9

SHOW YOUR WORK

Solve each problem.

10. There are 36 students who live in the college dormitory. If 4 students live in each room, how many rooms are there in the dormitory?

There are ________ rooms in the dormitory.

11. A package of 42 candies is evenly divided among 7 people. How many candies does each person receive?

Each person receives ________ candies.

12. A bookshelf contains 56 books. There are 7 shelves in the bookshelf. Each shelf has the same number of books on it. How many books are on each shelf?

There are ________ books on each shelf.

13. Eight people paid a total of 24 dollars for admission into the school carnival. If each ticket cost the same amount, how much did each ticket cost?

The cost of each ticket was ________ dollars.

14. A family of 5 takes an ice chest to the beach. There are 10 water bottles in the ice chest. How many water bottles will each person receive if each person receives the same number of water bottles?

Each person will receive ________ water bottles.

15. Eighteen fish were caught on a deep-sea fishing boat. If each person on the boat caught 2 fish, how many people were on the boat?

There were ________ people on the boat.

10.

11.

12.

13.

14.

15.

NAME ____________________

Lesson 6.1 Understanding Division

$\overline{)}$ means divide.

$$\text{divisor} \longrightarrow 3\overline{)18} \longleftarrow \text{dividend}, \quad 6 \longleftarrow \text{quotient}$$

$\begin{array}{r} 6 \\ 3\overline{)18} \end{array}$ is read "18 divided by 3 is equal to 6."

$\begin{array}{r} 3 \\ 4\overline{)12} \end{array}$ is read "12 divided by 4 is equal to 3."

In $\begin{array}{r} 3 \\ 4\overline{)12} \end{array}$, the divisor is 4, the dividend is 12, and the quotient is 3.

÷ also means divide.

$10 \div 2 = 5$ (10: dividend, 2: divisor, 5: quotient)

$10 \div 2 = 5$ is read "10 divided by 2 is equal to 5."

$6 \div 3 = 2$ is read "6 divided by 3 is equal to 2."

In $6 \div 3 = 2$, the divisor is 3, the dividend is 6, and the quotient is 2.

Complete each sentence.

1. $\begin{array}{r} 2 \\ 6\overline{)12} \end{array}$ is read "_12_ divided by 6 is equal to _2_."
2. $\begin{array}{r} 3 \\ 8\overline{)24} \end{array}$ is read "___ divided by 8 is equal to ___."
3. $\begin{array}{r} 9 \\ 4\overline{)36} \end{array}$ is read "___ divided by 4 is equal to ___."
4. In $\begin{array}{r} 2 \\ 4\overline{)8} \end{array}$, the divisor is ___, the dividend is ___, and the quotient is ___.
5. In $\begin{array}{r} 5 \\ 7\overline{)35} \end{array}$, the divisor is ___, the dividend is ___, and the quotient is ___.
6. $20 \div 5 = 4$ is read "___ divided by 5 is equal to ___."
7. $27 \div 9 = 3$ is read "___ divided by 9 is equal to ___."
8. $6 \div 2 = 3$ is read "___ divided by 2 is equal to ___."
9. In $15 \div 3 = 5$, the divisor is ___, the dividend is ___, and the quotient is ___.
10. In $14 \div 2 = 7$, the divisor is ___, the dividend is ___, and the quotient is ___.

NAME ____________________

Lesson 6.1 Understanding Division

8 △ in all.
4 △ in each group.
How many groups?
8 ÷ 4 = 2
There are 2 groups.

8 △ in all.
2 groups of △.
How many △ in each group?
8 ÷ 2 = 4
There are 4 in each group.

Check by multiplication: quotient × divisor = dividend.

2 × 4 = 8 4 × 2 = 8

Complete the following.

a

1. 12 □ in all.
3 □ in each group.
How many groups?
12 ÷ 3 = 4
There are 4 groups.
Check: 4 × 3 = 12

b

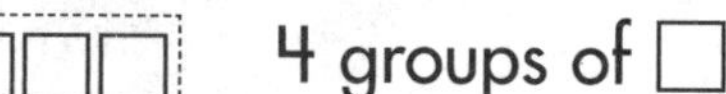

12 □ in all.
4 groups of □.
How many in each group?
12 ÷ 4 = ______
There are ______ □ in each group.
Check: ______________

2. 20 As in all.
______ As in each group.
How many groups?
20 ÷ 4 = ______
There are ______ groups.
Check: ______________

20 As in all.
______ groups of As.
How many in each group?
20 ÷ 5 = ______
There are ______ As in each group.
Check: ______________

3. ______ Fs in all.
______ Fs in each group.
How many groups?
12 ÷ 2 = ______
There are ______ groups.
Check: ______________

______ Fs in all.
______ groups of Fs.
How many in each group?
12 ÷ 6 = ______
There are ______ Fs in each group.
Check: ______________

NAME ___________________________

Lesson 6.2 Dividing through 27 ÷ 3

$$\begin{array}{r} 5 \\ \times\ 3 \\ \hline 15 \end{array} \longrightarrow 3\overline{)15}\text{ with quotient } 5$$

If 3 × 5 = 15, then 15 ÷ 3 = 5.

$$\begin{array}{r} 6 \\ \times\ 2 \\ \hline 12 \end{array} \longrightarrow 2\overline{)12}\text{ with quotient } 6$$

If 2 × 6 = 12, then 12 ÷ 2 = 6.

Divide. Under each division problem, write the corresponding multiplication problem.

	a	b	c	d	e
1.	$3\overline{)6}$ = 2 3 × 2 = 6	$2\overline{)14}$ = 7 2 × 7 = 14	$1\overline{)5}$	$2\overline{)4}$	$1\overline{)4}$
2.	$3\overline{)27}$	$1\overline{)3}$	$2\overline{)18}$	$1\overline{)7}$	$3\overline{)21}$
3.	$3\overline{)12}$	$2\overline{)16}$	$1\overline{)5}$	$3\overline{)18}$	$2\overline{)10}$
4.	$1\overline{)6}$	$1\overline{)8}$	$2\overline{)8}$	$1\overline{)2}$	$1\overline{)1}$
5.	$3\overline{)24}$	$3\overline{)9}$	$1\overline{)9}$	$2\overline{)6}$	$2\overline{)2}$

NAME ____________________

Lesson 6.2 Problem Solving

SHOW YOUR WORK

Solve each problem.

1. Joe's fish store has 18 goldfish. The fish are in 3 aquariums. The same number of goldfish are in each aquarium. How many goldfish are in each aquarium?

There are __________ goldfish.

There are __________ aquariums.

There are __________ goldfish in each aquarium.

2. Sally has 16 shoes in her closet. A pair of shoes is a group of 2 shoes. How many pairs of shoes does Sally have?

Sally has __________ shoes.

A pair is a group of __________ shoes.

Sally has __________ pairs of shoes.

3. The egg carton has 12 eggs in it. There are 2 rows in the carton. How many eggs are in each row?

The egg carton has __________ eggs.

There are __________ rows in the carton.

There are __________ eggs in each row.

4. Elisa has 15 sticks of gum. If she gives each of her 3 friends the same number of sticks of gum, how many sticks of gum will each of Elisa's friends have?

Each of Elisa's friends will have __________ sticks of gum.

5. Alvin earned 27 dollars for mowing 3 lawns on Saturday. Alvin earned the same amount of money for each lawn. How much did he earn for each lawn?

Alvin earned __________ dollars for each lawn he mowed.

1.	
2.	
3.	
4.	5.

NAME ______________________

Lesson 6.3 Dividing through 54 ÷ 6

$$\begin{array}{r} 5 \\ \times\ 4 \\ \hline 20 \end{array} \rightarrow 4\overline{)20}\ \text{quotient } 5$$

$$\begin{array}{r} 8 \\ \times\ 6 \\ \hline 48 \end{array} \rightarrow 6\overline{)48}\ \text{quotient } 8$$

If 4 × 5 = 20, then 20 ÷ 4 = 5.

If 6 × 8 = 48, then 48 ÷ 6 = 8.

Divide. Under each division problem write the corresponding multiplication problem.

	a	b	c	d	e
1.	$6\overline{)54}$ = 9 6 × 9 = 54	$3\overline{)27}$	$6\overline{)48}$	$5\overline{)25}$	$4\overline{)36}$
2.	$5\overline{)30}$	$4\overline{)24}$	$4\overline{)32}$	$4\overline{)16}$	$4\overline{)20}$

Divide.

	a	b	c	d	e
3.	$6\overline{)36}$	$4\overline{)28}$	$5\overline{)35}$	$6\overline{)24}$	$3\overline{)21}$
4.	$5\overline{)45}$	$6\overline{)12}$	$5\overline{)40}$	$3\overline{)24}$	$6\overline{)18}$
5.	$3\overline{)12}$	$2\overline{)16}$	$4\overline{)12}$	$2\overline{)18}$	$3\overline{)9}$
6.	$5\overline{)15}$	$6\overline{)42}$	$3\overline{)18}$	$6\overline{)6}$	$3\overline{)27}$

NAME ______________________

Lesson 6.3 Problem Solving

SHOW YOUR WORK

Solve each problem.

1. There are 24 hours in a day. If the day is divided into 6 equal time segments, how many hours will be in each time segment?

   There are __________ hours.

   There are __________ time segments.

   There are __________ hours in each time segment.

2. There are 30 desks in the classroom. There are 6 desks in each row. How many rows of desks are there?

   There are __________ desks.

   There are __________ desks in each row.

   There are __________ rows of desks.

3. Mr. Villa handed out 42 papers to 6 students. Each student received the same number of papers. How many papers did each student receive?

   Mr. Villa handed out __________ papers.

   There are __________ students.

   Each student received __________ papers.

4. There are 12 months in a year. There are 4 seasons in a year. If each season has an equal number of months, how many months are in each season?

   There are __________ months in each season.

5. Bianca has 48 roses. She has 6 vases. Bianca wants to put an equal number of roses in each vase. How many roses will Bianca put in each vase?

   Bianca will put __________ roses in each vase.

1.	
2.	
3.	
4.	5.

Lesson 6.4 Dividing through 81 ÷ 9

$$\begin{array}{r} 6 \\ \times\ 9 \\ \hline 54 \end{array} \quad 9\overline{)54} \text{ with answer } 6$$

$$\begin{array}{r} 9 \\ \times\ 7 \\ \hline 63 \end{array} \quad 7\overline{)63} \text{ with answer } 9$$

If 9 × 6 = 54, then 54 ÷ 9 = 6. If 7 × 9 = 63, then 63 ÷ 7 = 9.

Divide. Under each division problem write the corresponding multiplication problem.

	a	b	c	d	e
1.	7)7 (answer: 1) 7 × 1 = 7	6)24	8)56	6)30	8)64
2.	6)12	7)35	8)24	7)28	6)36

Divide.

	a	b	c	d	e
3.	9)63	9)81	7)56	5)35	8)24
4.	9)18	7)14	7)21	8)48	9)45
5.	7)49	8)16	9)27	9)9	7)42
6.	9)27	9)54	8)8	6)54	8)40

NAME ___________________________

Lesson 6.4 Problem Solving

SHOW YOUR WORK

Solve each problem.

1. Spencer wants to save 72 dollars. How many weeks will it take Spencer to save 72 dollars if he saves 9 dollars each week?

Spencer wants to save __________ dollars.

He saves __________ dollars each week.

It will take Spencer __________ weeks to save 72 dollars.

2. Ms. Jefferson worked 40 hours this week. She worked 8 hours each day. How many days did she work this week?

Ms. Jefferson worked __________ hours this week.

She worked __________ hours each day.

She worked __________ days this week.

3. There are 16 football players on the field. If there are 8 players on each team, how many teams are on the field?

There are __________ football players on the field.

There are __________ players on each team.

There are __________ teams on the field.

4. Mrs. Daniels ordered 63 tables and 7 chairs for a banquet. Each table will have the same number of chairs. How many chairs will be at each table?

There will be __________ chairs at each table.

1.

2.

3.

4.

NAME ______________________

Lesson 6.5 Division Practice

Divide.

	a	b	c	d	e
1.	5)25	4)16	7)21	9)81	6)18
2.	6)54	3)27	9)72	7)49	5)5
3.	3)24	4)28	9)36	2)14	1)9
4.	3)6	8)16	7)35	5)15	3)9
5.	7)42	9)45	2)2	7)63	2)6
6.	5)20	2)18	8)32	4)24	8)72
7.	1)1	8)64	6)36	5)45	2)16
8.	8)48	3)15	3)21	9)54	1)5
9.	8)24	7)28	4)36	7)14	9)9
10.	5)35	6)42	5)45	1)2	9)63

NAME ______________________

Lesson 6.6 Division and Multiplication Practice

Divide or multiply.

	a	b	c	d	e	f
1.	$3\overline{)6}$	$9\overline{)18}$	$4\overline{)36}$	$6\overline{)54}$	$3\overline{)27}$	$2\overline{)4}$
2.	$8\overline{)40}$	$3\overline{)18}$	$2\overline{)6}$	$3\overline{)9}$	$2\overline{)16}$	$5\overline{)20}$
3.	$4\overline{)32}$	$9\overline{)27}$	$2\overline{)8}$	$1\overline{)7}$	$5\overline{)5}$	$9\overline{)54}$
4.	$7\overline{)42}$	$6\overline{)12}$	$9\overline{)81}$	$4\overline{)4}$	$6\overline{)24}$	$2\overline{)10}$
5.	$1\overline{)2}$	$4\overline{)20}$	$3\overline{)15}$	$6\overline{)48}$	$3\overline{)12}$	$8\overline{)56}$
6.	86×3	72×5	67×4	91×9	22×7	10×6
7.	51×2	38×7	43×8	29×1	18×6	97×3
8.	7×6	16×9	82×5	33×3	17×8	56×2
9.	13×6	10×7	73×5	64×8	31×9	9×2
10.	53×8	76×4	21×7	89×2	47×5	28×9

NAME ______________________

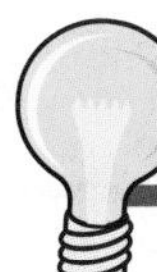

Check What You Learned

Division Facts through 81 ÷ 9

Divide.

	a	b	c	d	e
1.	$1\overline{)4}$	$2\overline{)16}$	$9\overline{)63}$	$7\overline{)42}$	$5\overline{)20}$
2.	$9\overline{)54}$	$9\overline{)9}$	$4\overline{)12}$	$1\overline{)6}$	$9\overline{)36}$
3.	$8\overline{)16}$	$5\overline{)25}$	$2\overline{)12}$	$4\overline{)8}$	$3\overline{)6}$
4.	$8\overline{)8}$	$6\overline{)30}$	$6\overline{)18}$	$6\overline{)54}$	$9\overline{)27}$
5.	$2\overline{)14}$	$2\overline{)10}$	$1\overline{)3}$	$4\overline{)20}$	$3\overline{)18}$
6.	$8\overline{)72}$	$2\overline{)6}$	$7\overline{)56}$	$3\overline{)24}$	$4\overline{)32}$
7.	$7\overline{)63}$	$4\overline{)16}$	$8\overline{)32}$	$5\overline{)30}$	$2\overline{)8}$
8.	$7\overline{)7}$	$8\overline{)24}$	$3\overline{)27}$	$6\overline{)6}$	$1\overline{)8}$
9.	$5\overline{)35}$	$6\overline{)42}$	$6\overline{)36}$	$8\overline{)64}$	$3\overline{)21}$

CHAPTER 6 POSTTEST

NAME ___________________________

Check What You Learned

SHOW YOUR WORK

Division Facts through 81 ÷ 9

CHAPTER 6 POSTTEST

Solve each problem.

10. There are 64 pages in a book. There are 8 chapters in the book. Each chapter has the same number of pages. How many pages are in each chapter of the book?

There are __________ pages in each chapter of the book.

11. Six horses can live in the stable. If 1 horse can live in each stall, how many stalls are in the stable?

There are __________ stalls in the stable.

12. A golfer shot a score of 45 in a golf match. She played 9 holes. She had the same score at each of the holes. What was her score at each hole?

She shot a score of __________ at each hole.

13. A package of 12 donuts was shared evenly among 3 friends. How many donuts did each friend receive?

Each friend received __________ donuts.

14. A bicycle has 18 speeds. Each of its 2 gears has the same number of speeds. How many speeds does the bicycle have for each gear?

Each gear has __________ speeds.

15. Forty teenagers went on a river-rafting trip. If each raft held 8 teenagers, how many rafts did the teenagers have for their trip?

The teenagers had __________ rafts.

10.

11.

12.

13.

14. **15.**

NAME ____________________

Mid-Test Chapters 1–6

Add or subtract.

	a	b	c	d	e
1.	5 +3	7 +12	33 + 2	19 + 7	21 + 5
2.	54 +13	16 +42	96 +39	16 +54	87 +63
3.	116 + 23	110 + 30	319 +400	607 +401	632 +481
4.	23 39 +42	11 31 +73	29 36 + 5	192 305 +486	611 812 +233
5.	53 −13	49 −23	16 − 9	29 −21	18 − 2
6.	36 −19	25 −16	85 −14	92 −33	45 −26
7.	511 − 31	206 − 92	554 − 41	592 − 51	793 − 82
8.	300 −200	596 −485	311 −120	529 −153	697 −593

CHAPTERS 1–6 MID-TEST

NAME ____________________

Mid-Test Chapters 1–6

Add or subtract.

	a	b	c	d	e
9.	1034 + 311	6654 + 2862	5112 + 3342	5762 + 2903	4863 + 2971
10.	7107 + 1986	5403 + 1969	4321 + 2642	1969 + 2543	6032 + 2961
11.	5110 − 210	8692 − 451	9893 − 4541	6103 − 5002	3000 − 1000
12.	5106 − 320	7980 − 990	6457 − 4366	9875 − 1994	8764 − 3873

Round each number to the place named.

	a	b	c	d	e
13.	5,432 tens	986 tens	78,654 hundreds	9,865 tens	54,329 thousands

Write each number in expanded form.

	a	b	c	d
14.	50,462	19,783	543	10,030

Compare each pair of numbers. Write <, >, or =.

	a	b	c	d	e
15.	32 ___ 93	110 ___ 110	54 ___ 52	16 ___ 61	103 ___ 13

NAME ______________________

Mid-Test Chapters 1–6

Multiply.

	a	b	c	d	e
16.	5×5	6×1	29×5	8×7	6×3
17.	84×3	9×7	6×5	44×2	39×1
18.	7×6	17×3	34×5	53×2	9×8
19.	15×4	62×3	19×3	2×4	23×4

Divide.

	a	b	c	d	e
20.	$6\overline{)18}$	$9\overline{)54}$	$8\overline{)48}$	$4\overline{)8}$	$6\overline{)6}$
21.	$9\overline{)81}$	$9\overline{)63}$	$2\overline{)16}$	$7\overline{)14}$	$6\overline{)36}$
22.	$9\overline{)18}$	$7\overline{)7}$	$6\overline{)12}$	$3\overline{)27}$	$8\overline{)24}$
23.	$3\overline{)21}$	$2\overline{)4}$	$4\overline{)32}$	$1\overline{)5}$	$9\overline{)27}$

CHAPTERS 1–6 MID-TEST

NAME ___________________________

Mid-Test Chapters 1–6

SHOW YOUR WORK

Solve each problem.

24. Sarah has 50 marbles and Jessie has 63 marbles. How many marbles do they have together?

Sarah and Jessie have _______ marbles together.

25. A pencil costs 48 cents and a package of gum costs 29 cents. Estimate about how much the pencil and the package of gum cost together.

The pencil and the package of gum cost about

_______ cents.

26. Gloria has saved 329 dollars. If she spends 58 dollars, how much money will she have left?

Gloria will have _______ dollars left.

27. Tito read 320 pages in a book. Akando read 323 pages in a book. Kenji read 313 pages in a book. How many pages did they read?

Tito, Akando, and Kenji read _______ pages.

28. In the year 1983, Mr. Smith was 94 years old. In what year was he born?

Mr. Smith was born in the year _______.

29. Tobias gave each of his 7 friends 4 baseball cards. How many baseball cards did Tobias give to his friends?

Tobias gave _______ trading cards to his friends.

30. Thirty-five people want to go camping. If each campsite can have a maximum of 7 people, what is the fewest number of campsites needed?

The least number of campsites needed is _______.

24.	25.
26.	27.
28.	29.
30.	

NAME ______________________

Check What You Know

Fractions

What fraction of each figure is shaded?

	a	b	c
1.	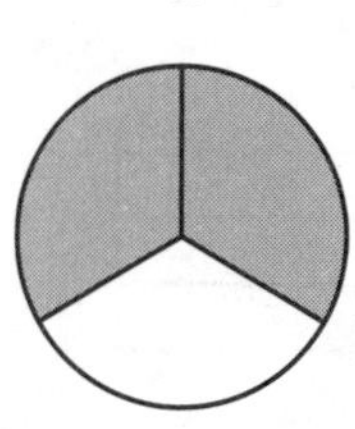 ________	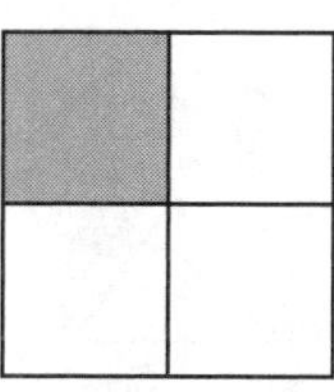 ________	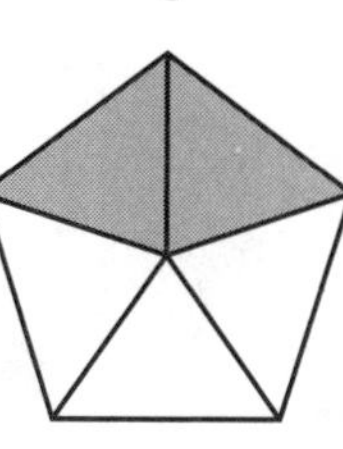 ________
2.	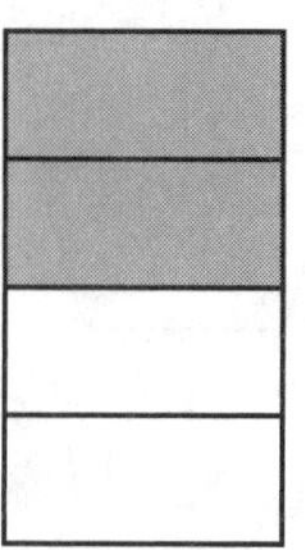 ________	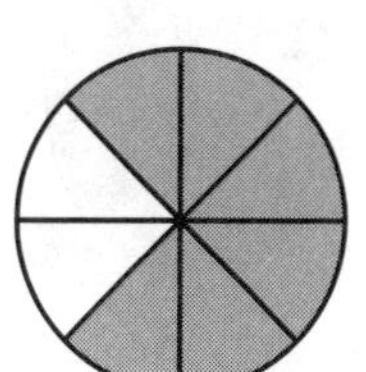 ________	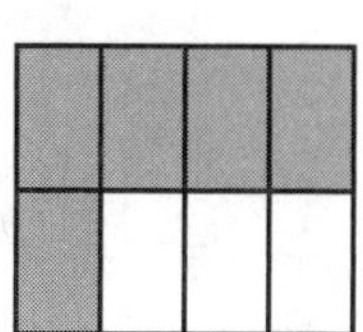 ________

What fraction of each set is shaded?

	a	b	c
3.	 ________	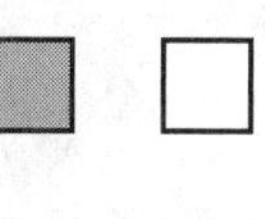 ________	 ________
4.	 ________	________	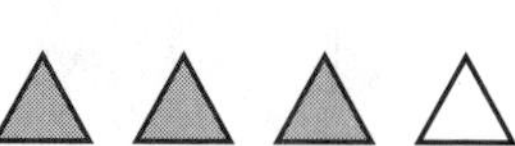 ________

NAME ________________

Check What You Know

Fractions

Use >, <, or = to compare the fractions.

	a		b		c	
5.	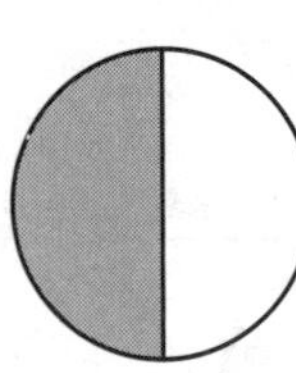		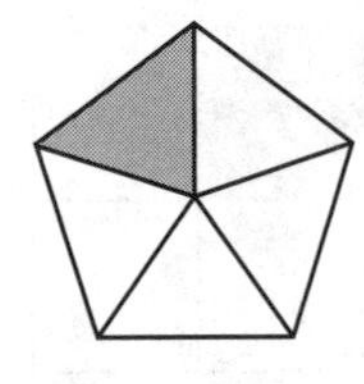		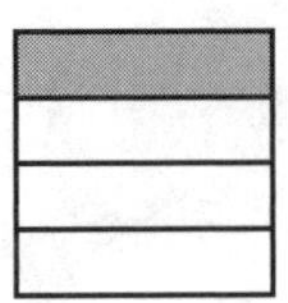	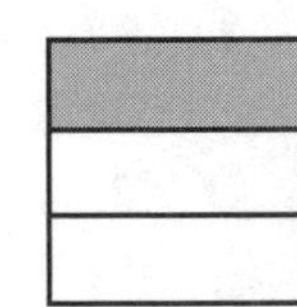
	$\frac{1}{2}$ ◯ $\frac{1}{4}$		$\frac{1}{5}$ ◯ $\frac{2}{5}$		$\frac{1}{4}$ ◯ $\frac{1}{3}$	
6.	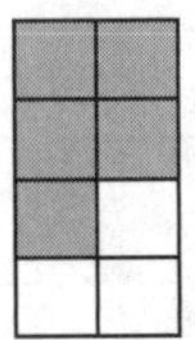 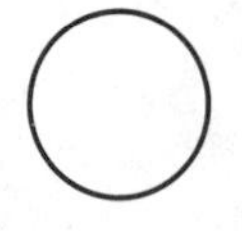		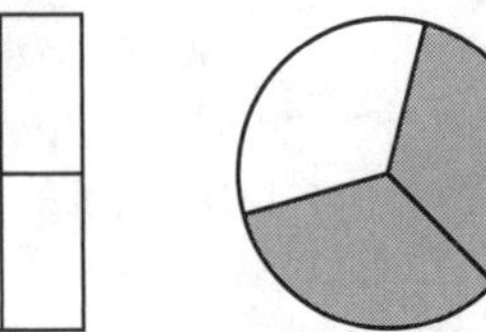  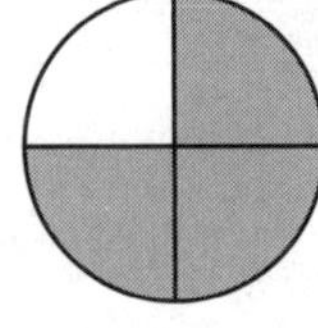		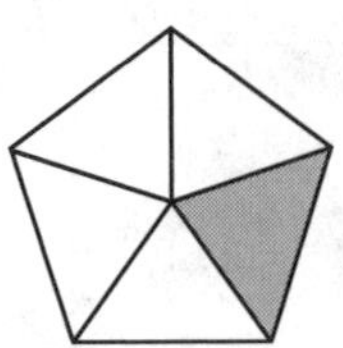 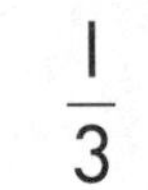 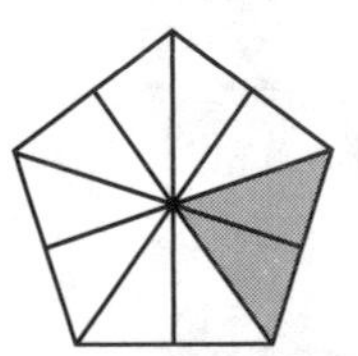	
	$\frac{5}{8}$ ◯ $\frac{1}{4}$		$\frac{2}{3}$ ◯ $\frac{3}{4}$		$\frac{1}{5}$ ◯ $\frac{2}{10}$	

What fraction of each figure is shaded? Compare the fractions. Use >, <, or =.

	a	b	c
7.	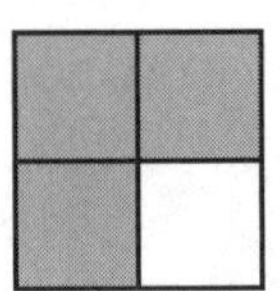	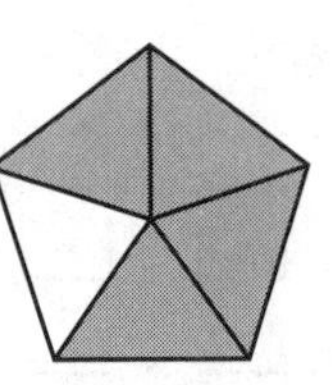 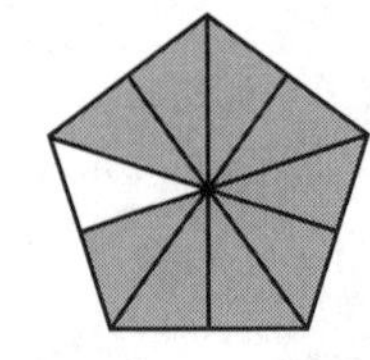	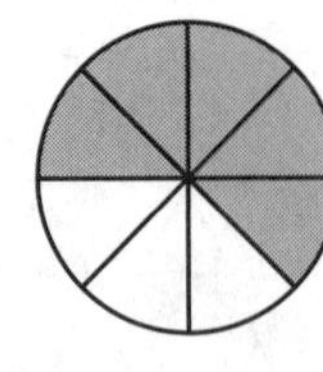 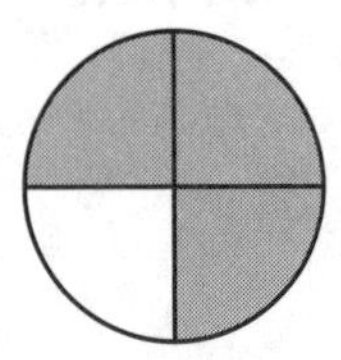
	____ ◯ ____	____ ◯ ____	____ ◯ ____
8.	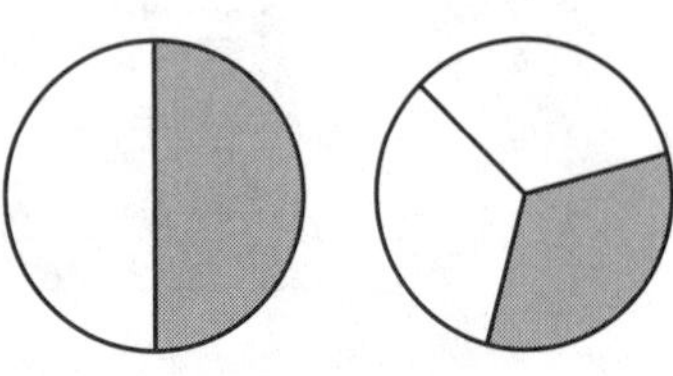	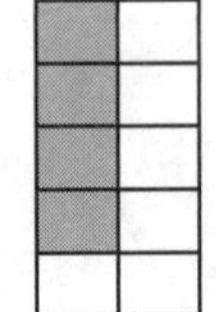 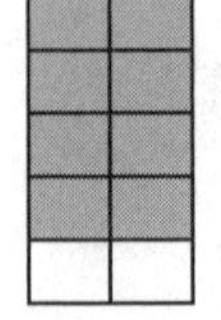	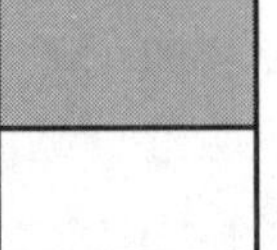 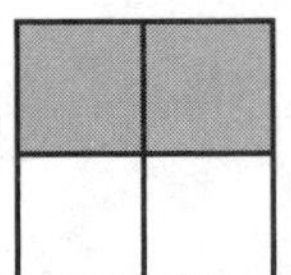
	____ ◯ ____	____ ◯ ____	____ ◯ ____

NAME ______________________________

Lesson 7.1 Parts of a Whole

A fraction is a number for part of a whole.

1 ⟵ numerator (part of the whole)
4 ⟵ denominator (parts in all)

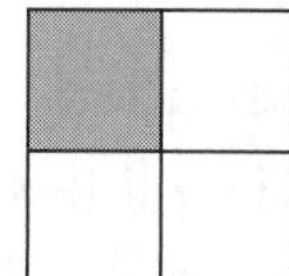

1 ⟵ part shaded
4 ⟵ parts in all

$\frac{1}{4}$ of the square is shaded.

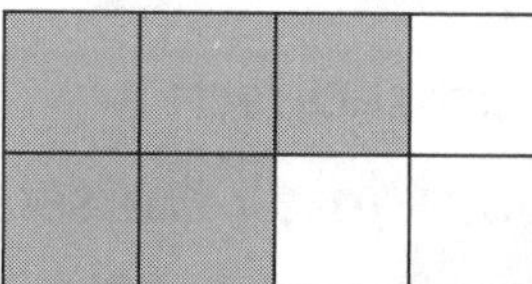

5 ⟵ parts shaded
8 ⟵ parts in all

$\frac{5}{8}$ of the rectangle is shaded.

What fraction of each figure is shaded?

	a	b	c
1.	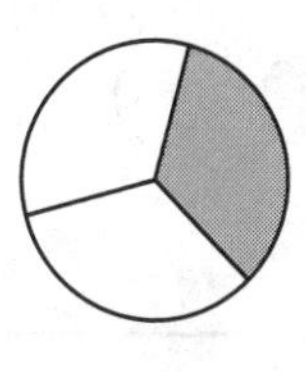 $\frac{1}{3}$ ________	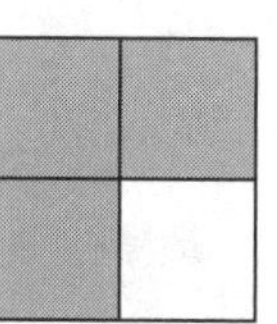 ________	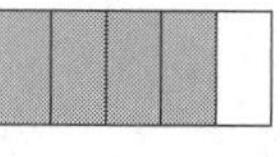 ________
2.	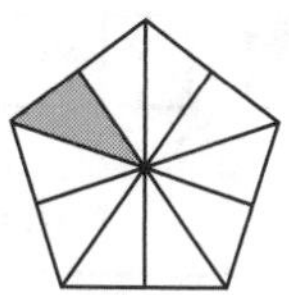 ________	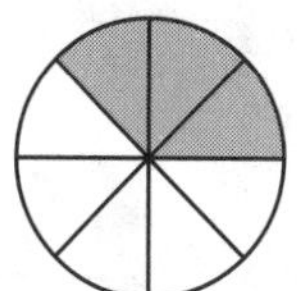 ________	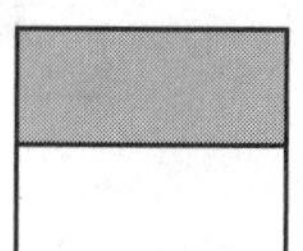 ________
3.	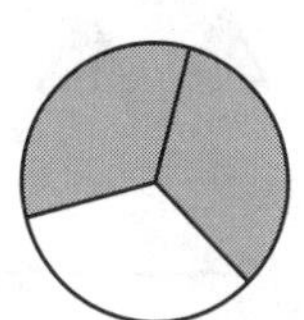 ________	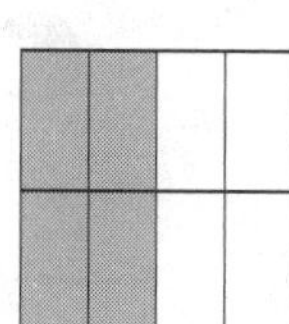 ________	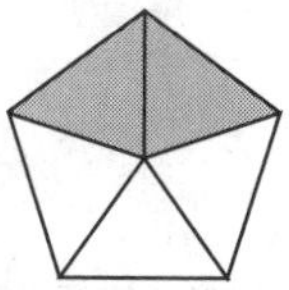 ________
4.	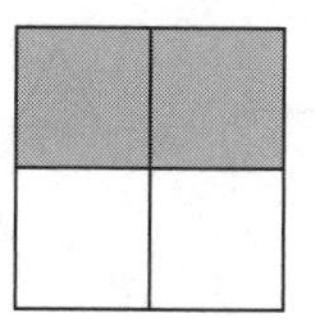 ________	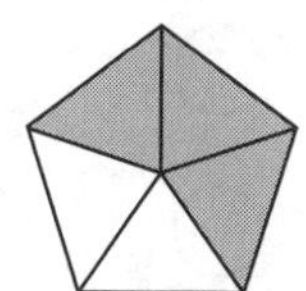 ________	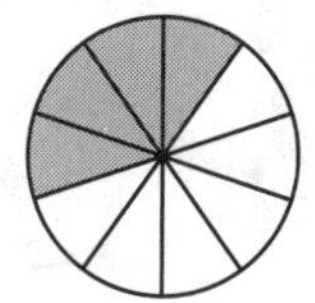 ________

NAME ____________________

Lesson 7.2 Parts of a Set

A fraction is a number for part of a set.

$\frac{1}{2}$ ← numerator (part of the set) ← denominator (parts in all the set)

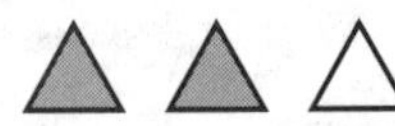

$\frac{1}{2}$ ← part shaded ← parts in all the set

$\frac{2}{3}$ ← parts shaded ← parts in all the set

What fraction of each set is shaded?

	a	b	c
1.	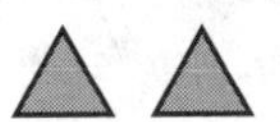 $\frac{4}{5}$	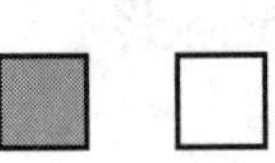 ______	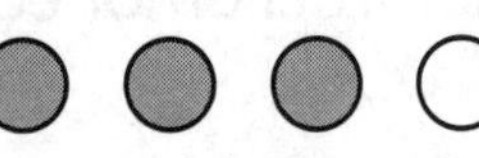 ______
2.	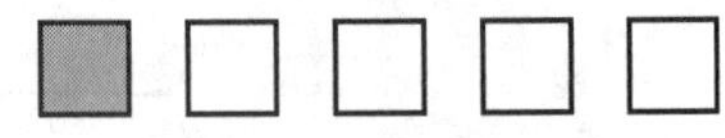 ______	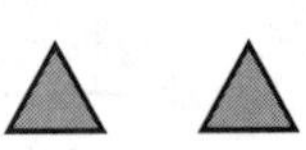 ______	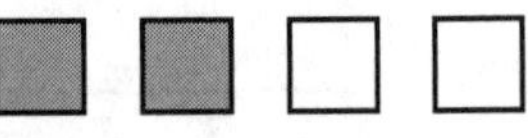 ______
3.	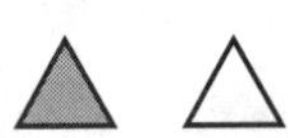 ______	 ______	 ______

Shade the number indicated by the fraction.

	a	b	c	d
4.	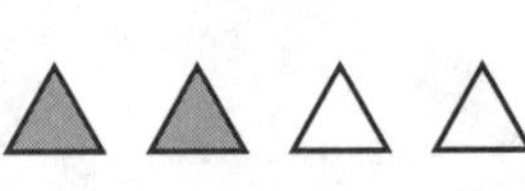 $\frac{4}{8}$	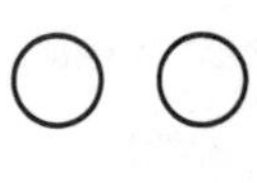 $\frac{3}{4}$	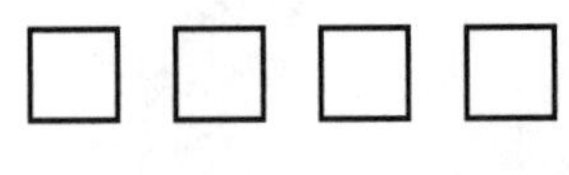 $\frac{3}{10}$	$\frac{1}{5}$

Lesson 7.3 Comparing Fractions

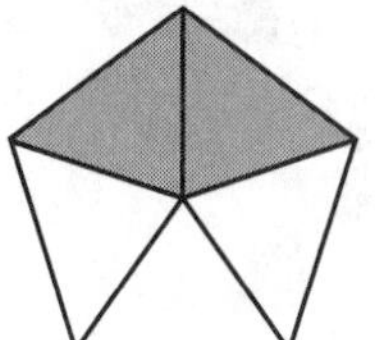
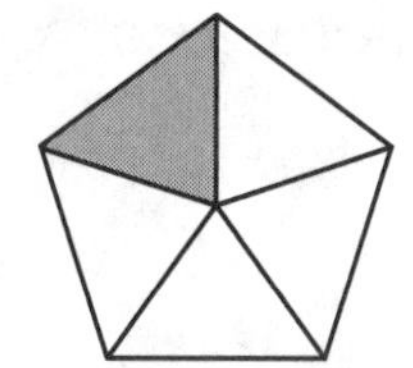
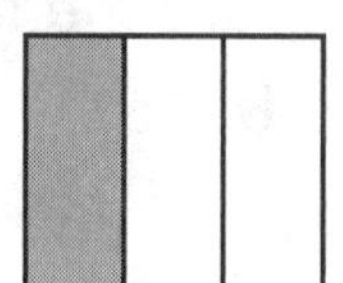
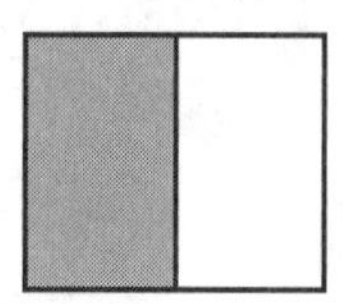
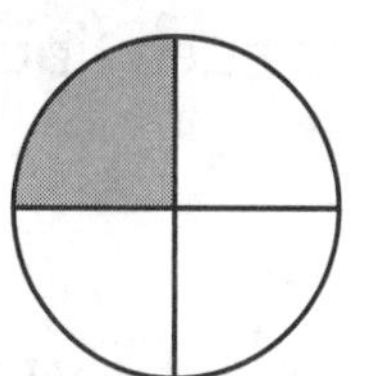
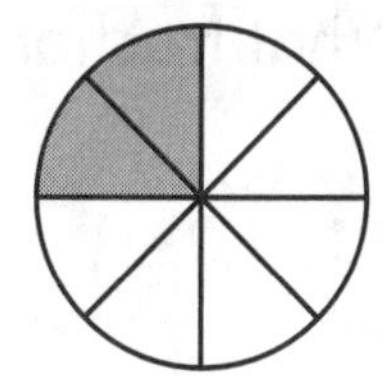

$\frac{2}{5} > \frac{1}{5}$ $\frac{1}{3} < \frac{1}{2}$ $\frac{1}{4} = \frac{2}{8}$

$\frac{2}{5}$ is greater than $\frac{1}{5}$. $\frac{1}{3}$ is less than $\frac{1}{2}$. $\frac{1}{4}$ is equal to $\frac{2}{8}$.

Use $>$, $<$, or $=$ to compare the fractions.

	a	b	c
1.	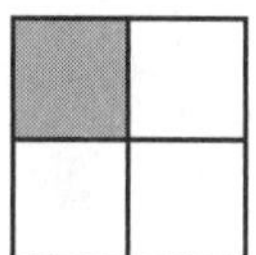 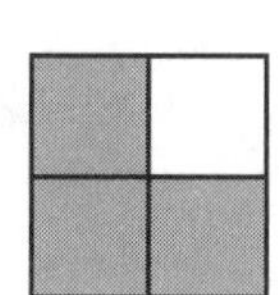 $\frac{1}{4}$ ($<$) $\frac{3}{4}$	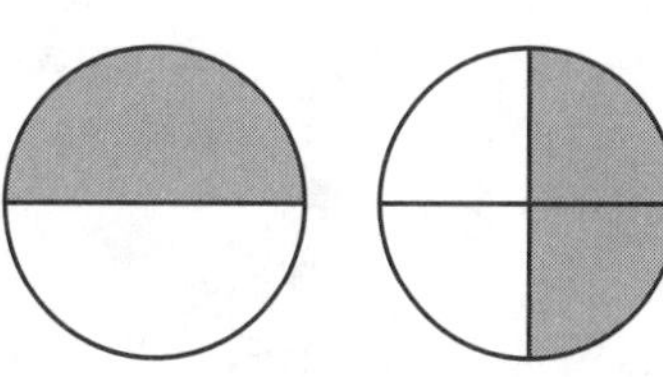 $\frac{1}{2}$ ◯ $\frac{2}{4}$	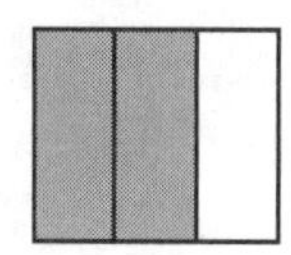 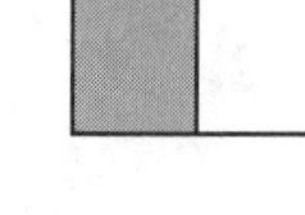 $\frac{2}{3}$ ◯ $\frac{1}{2}$
2.	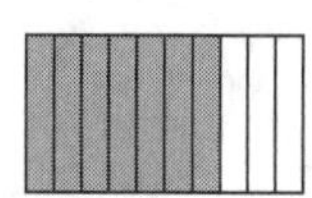 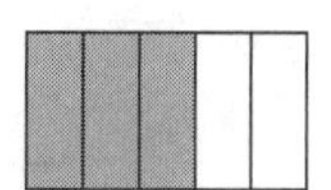 $\frac{7}{10}$ ◯ $\frac{3}{5}$	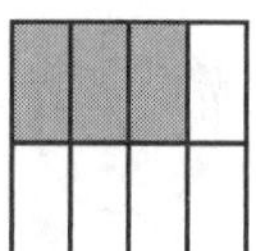 $\frac{3}{8}$ ◯ $\frac{3}{4}$	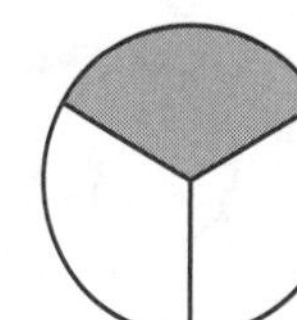 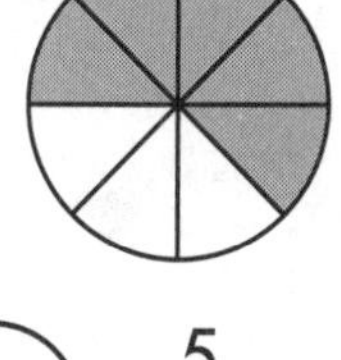 $\frac{1}{3}$ ◯ $\frac{5}{8}$
3.	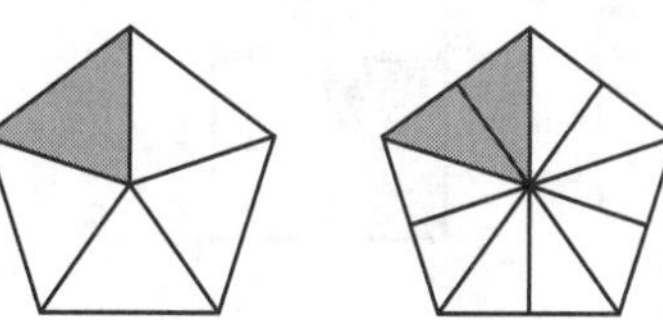 $\frac{1}{5}$ ◯ $\frac{2}{10}$	 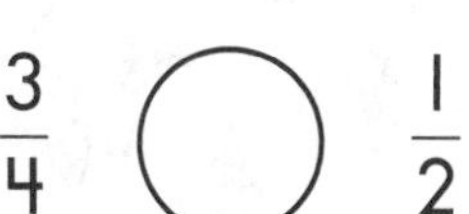 $\frac{3}{4}$ ◯ $\frac{1}{2}$	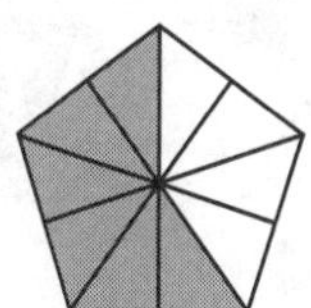 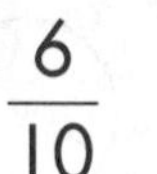 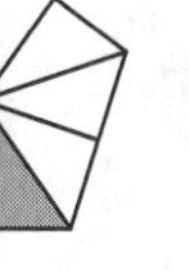 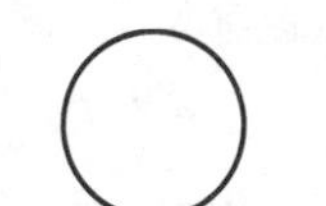 $\frac{6}{10}$ ◯ $\frac{2}{5}$

NAME ___________________________

Lesson 7.3 Comparing Fractions

What fraction of each figure is shaded? Compare the fractions. Use >, <, or = .

a **b** **c**

1.

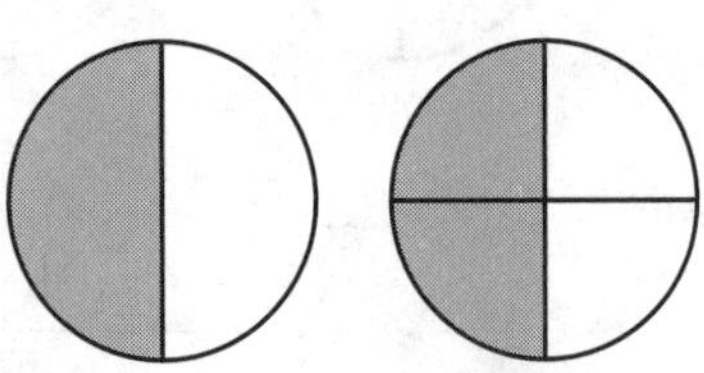

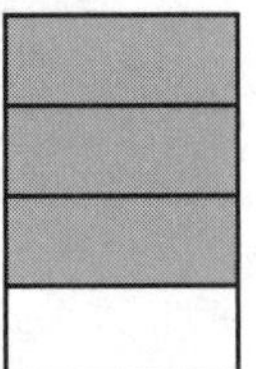

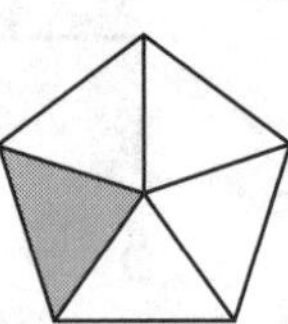

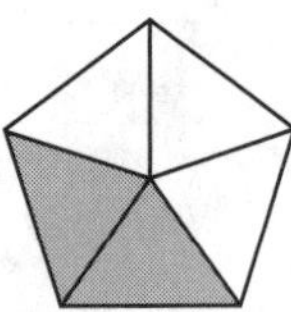

$\frac{1}{2}$ (=) $\frac{2}{4}$ 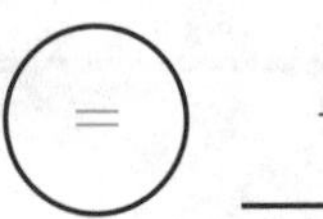

____ ( ) ____ 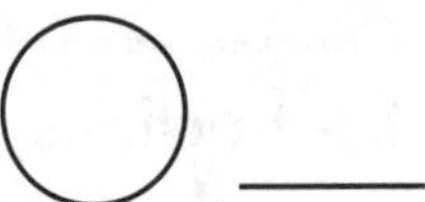

____ ( ) ____

2.

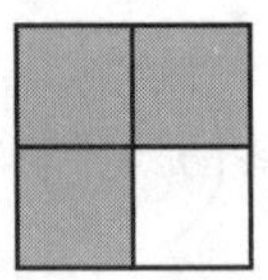

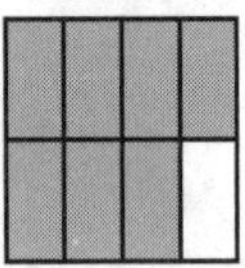

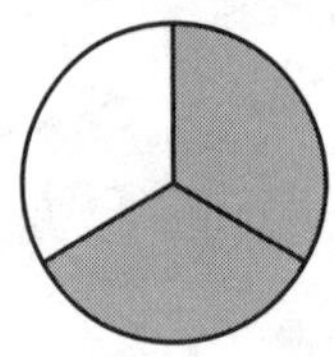

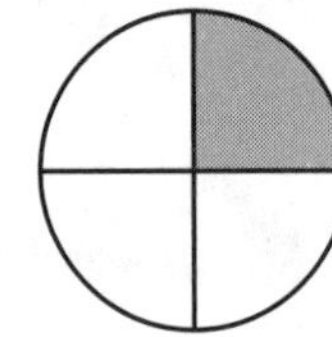

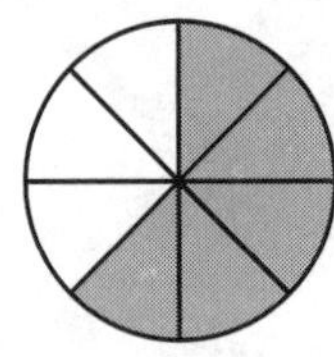

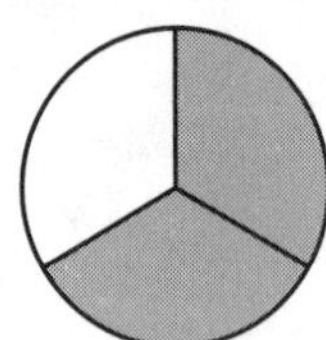

____ ( ) ____   ____ ( ) ____   ____ ( ) ____ 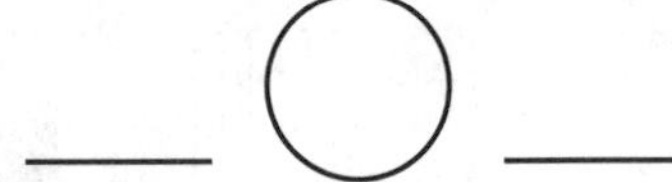

3.

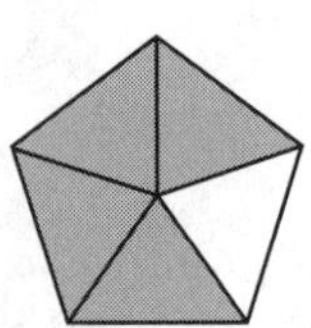

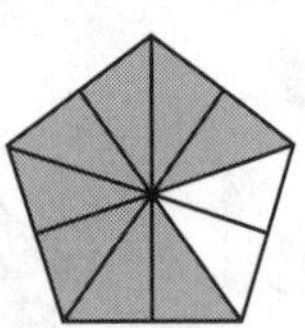

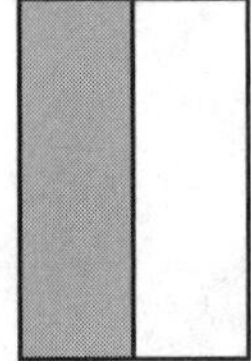

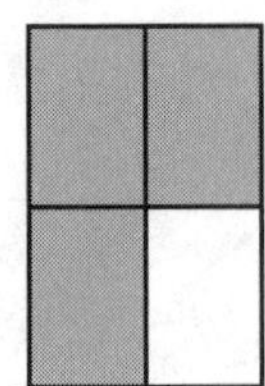

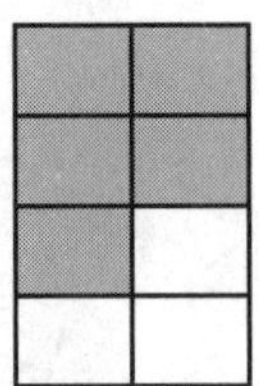

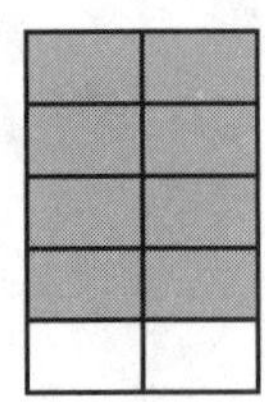

____ ( ) ____   ____ ( ) ____ 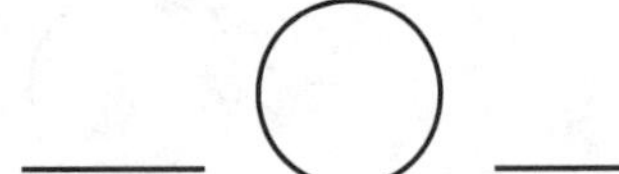   ____ ( ) ____ 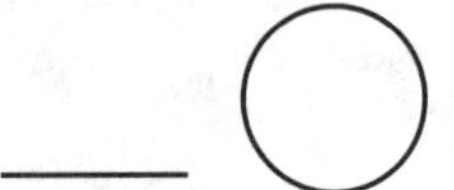

NAME ______________________

Check What You Learned

Fractions

What fraction of each figure is shaded?

	a	b	c
1.	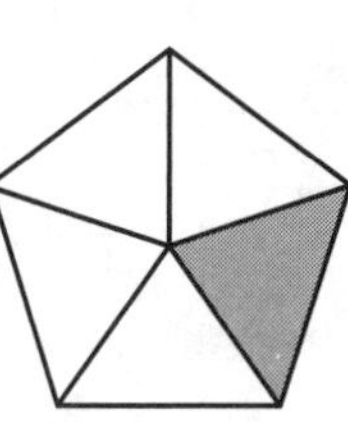 ______	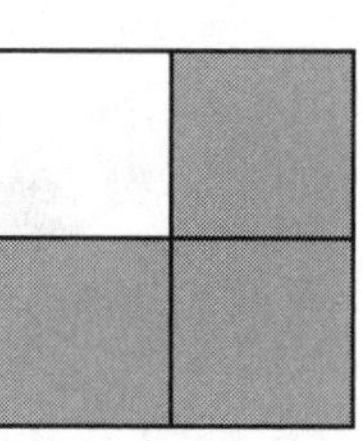 ______	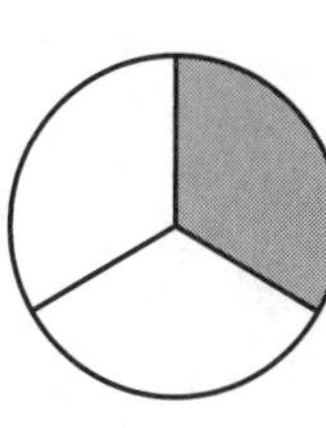 ______
2.	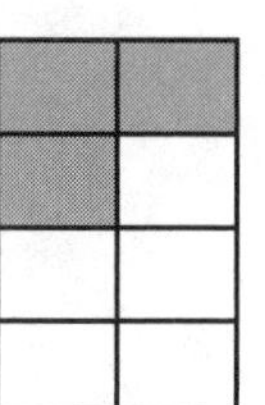 ______	______	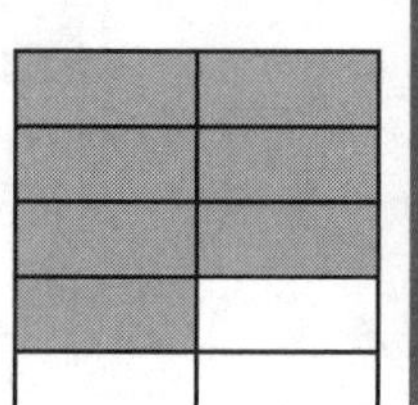 ______

CHAPTER 7 POSTTEST

What fraction of each set is shaded?

	a	b	c
3.	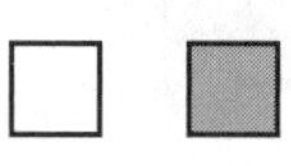 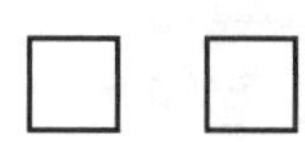 ______	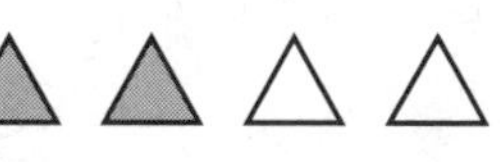 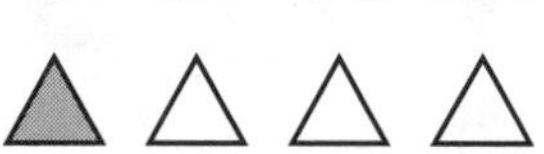 ______	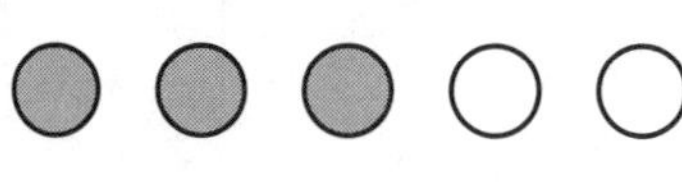  ______
4.	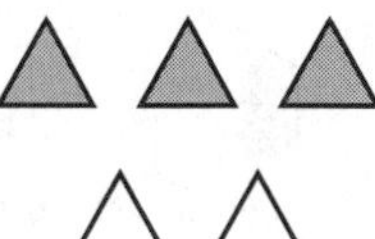 ______	______	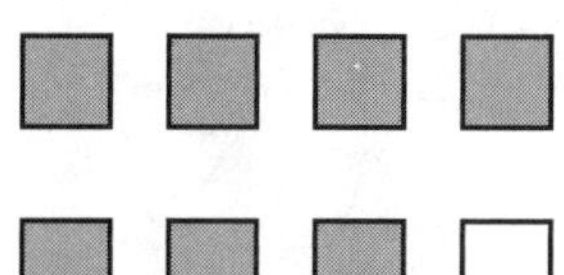 ______

NAME ____________________

Check What You Learned

Fractions

Use >, <, or = to compare the fractions.

	a	b	c
5.	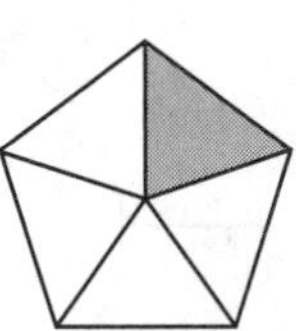 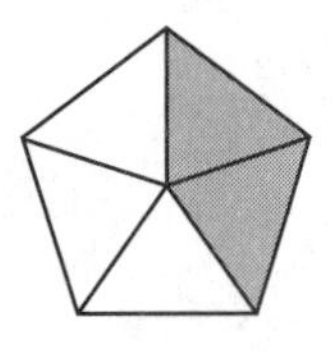 $\frac{1}{5}$ ◯ $\frac{2}{5}$	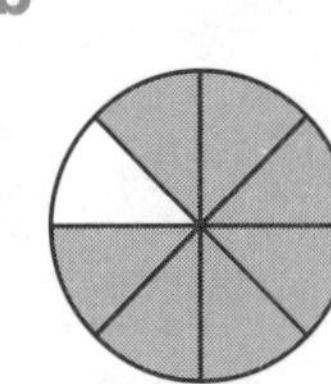 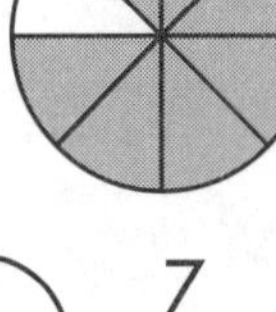 $\frac{1}{3}$ ◯ $\frac{7}{8}$	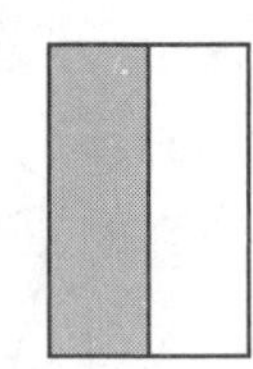 $\frac{4}{8}$ ◯ $\frac{1}{2}$
6.	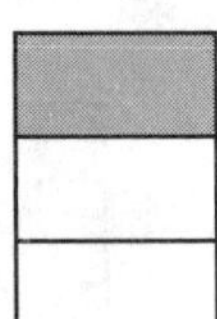 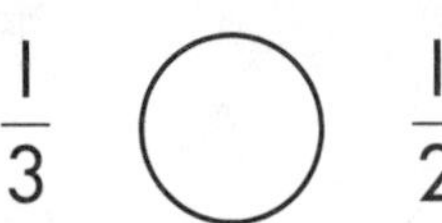 $\frac{1}{3}$ ◯ $\frac{1}{2}$	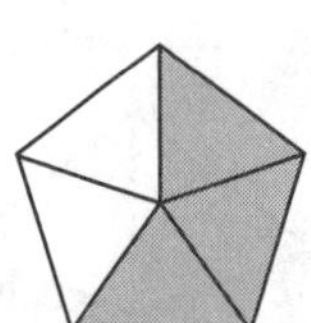 $\frac{3}{5}$ ◯ $\frac{2}{10}$	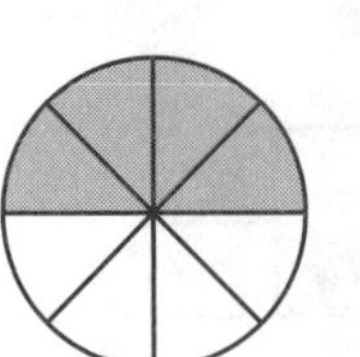 $\frac{4}{8}$ ◯ $\frac{2}{4}$

CHAPTER 7 POSTTEST

What fraction of each figure is shaded? Compare the fractions. Use >, <, or =.

	a	b	c
7.	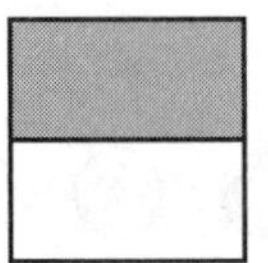  ____ ◯ ____	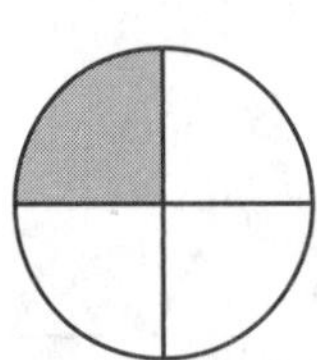 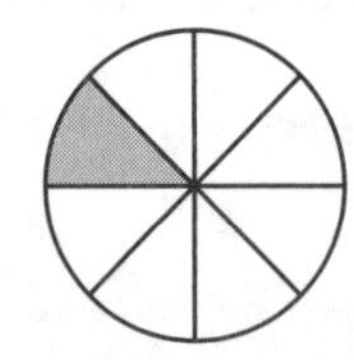 ____ ◯ ____	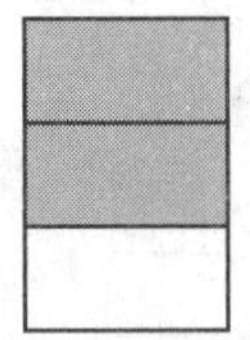 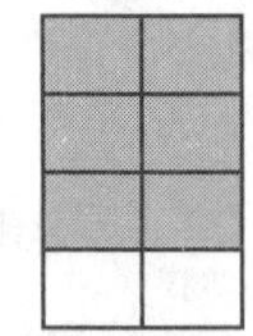 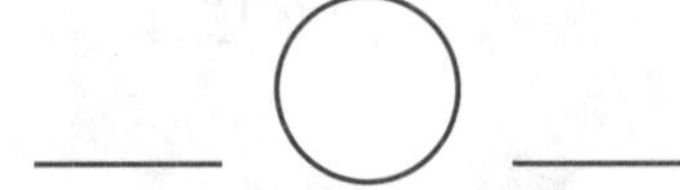 ____ ◯ ____
8.	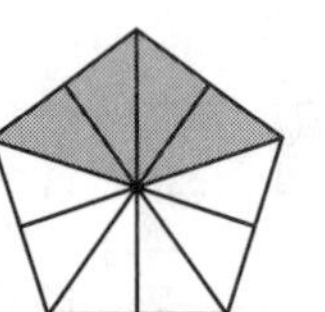 ____ ◯ ____	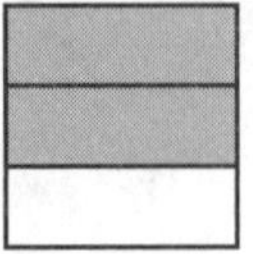 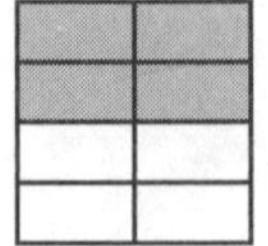 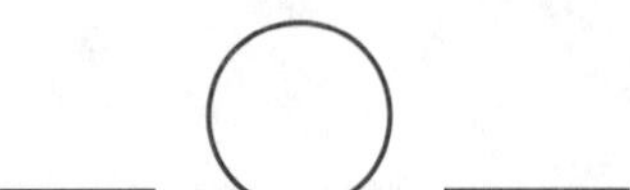 ____ ◯ ____	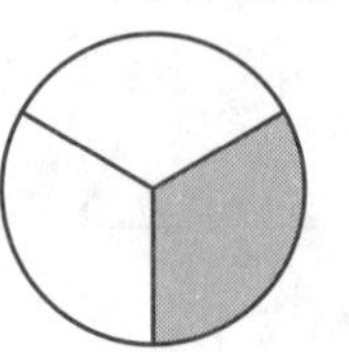 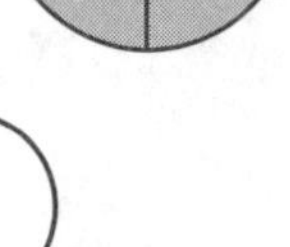 ____ ◯ ____

NAME ____________________

Check What You Know

Customary Measurement

CHAPTER 8 PRETEST

Use a ruler to find the length of each object to the nearest inch.

1. __________ in.

2. __________ in.

3. __________ in.

SHOW YOUR WORK

Solve each problem.

4. The rope is 27 feet long. How long is the rope in yards?

   The rope is __________ yards long.

5. The book is 12 inches wide. What is the width of the book in feet?

   The book is __________ foot wide.

6. At an amusement park, Andrea needs to be 48 inches tall to ride the roller coaster. Andrea is 4 feet tall. Can she ride the roller coaster?

   Andrea __________ ride the roller coaster.

7. A cookie recipe calls for 8 ounces of butter. Ryan has 1 pound of butter. Does he have enough butter to make cookies?

   Ryan __________ enough butter to make cookies.

8. Sue has 3 gallons of orange juice. How many cups of orange juice does she have?

   Sue has __________ cups of orange juice.

4.

5.

6.

7.

8.

NAME ____________________

CHAPTER 8 PRETEST

Check What You Know

Customary Measurement

SHOW YOUR WORK

Solve each problem.

9. A bag of fruit weighs 32 ounces. How many pounds does this bag of fruit weigh?

   The bag of fruit weighs ________ pounds.

10. Which weighs more, 20 ounces or 1 pound?

    ________ weighs more.

11. Would you measure a feather in ounces or in pounds?

    You would measure a feather in ________.

12. Would you measure the length of a jump rope in inches or feet?

    You would measure a jump rope in ________.

13. Would you measure the gasoline in a truck in cups, pints, quarts, or gallons?

    You would measure the gasoline in a truck in ________.

14. Would you measure juice in a pitcher by cups or quarts?

    You would measure the juice in a pitcher in ________.

15. Four quarts is equal to how many pints?

    Four quarts is equal to ________ pints.

16. The thermometer read 93° Fahrenheit at noon. At 5:00 p.m. the thermometer read 80° Fahrenheit. From noon until 5:00 p.m., how much did the temperature decrease?

    The temperature decreased ________ °F.

9.	10.
11.	12.
13.	14.
15.	16.

NAME ____________________

Lesson 8.1 Measuring in Inches

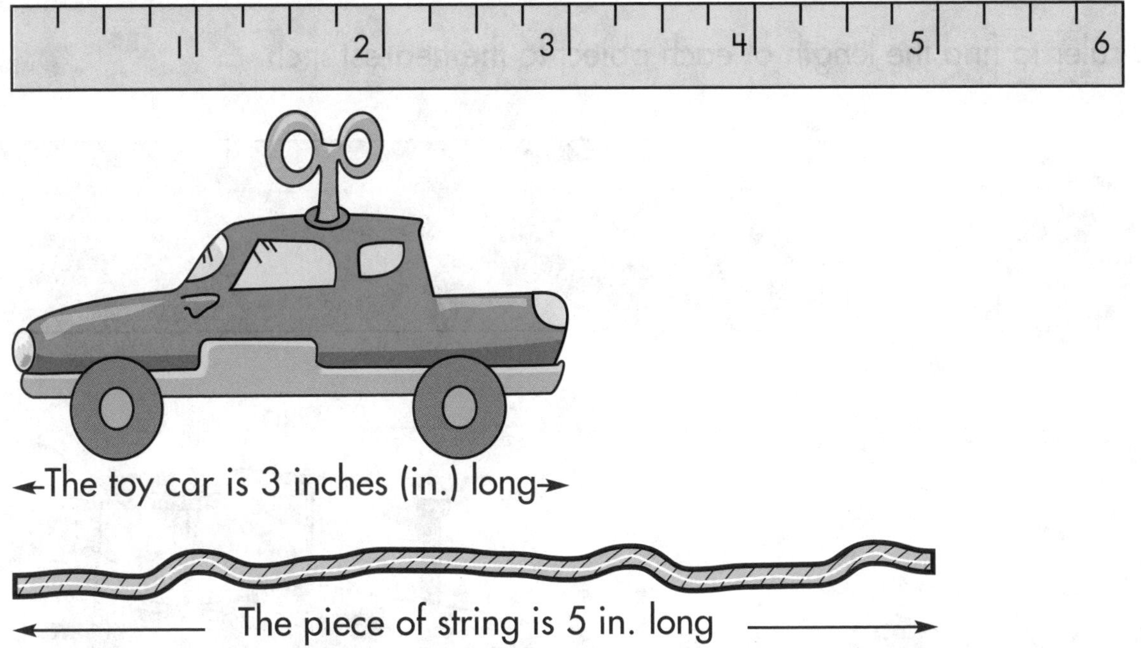

Use a ruler to find the length of each object to the nearest inch.

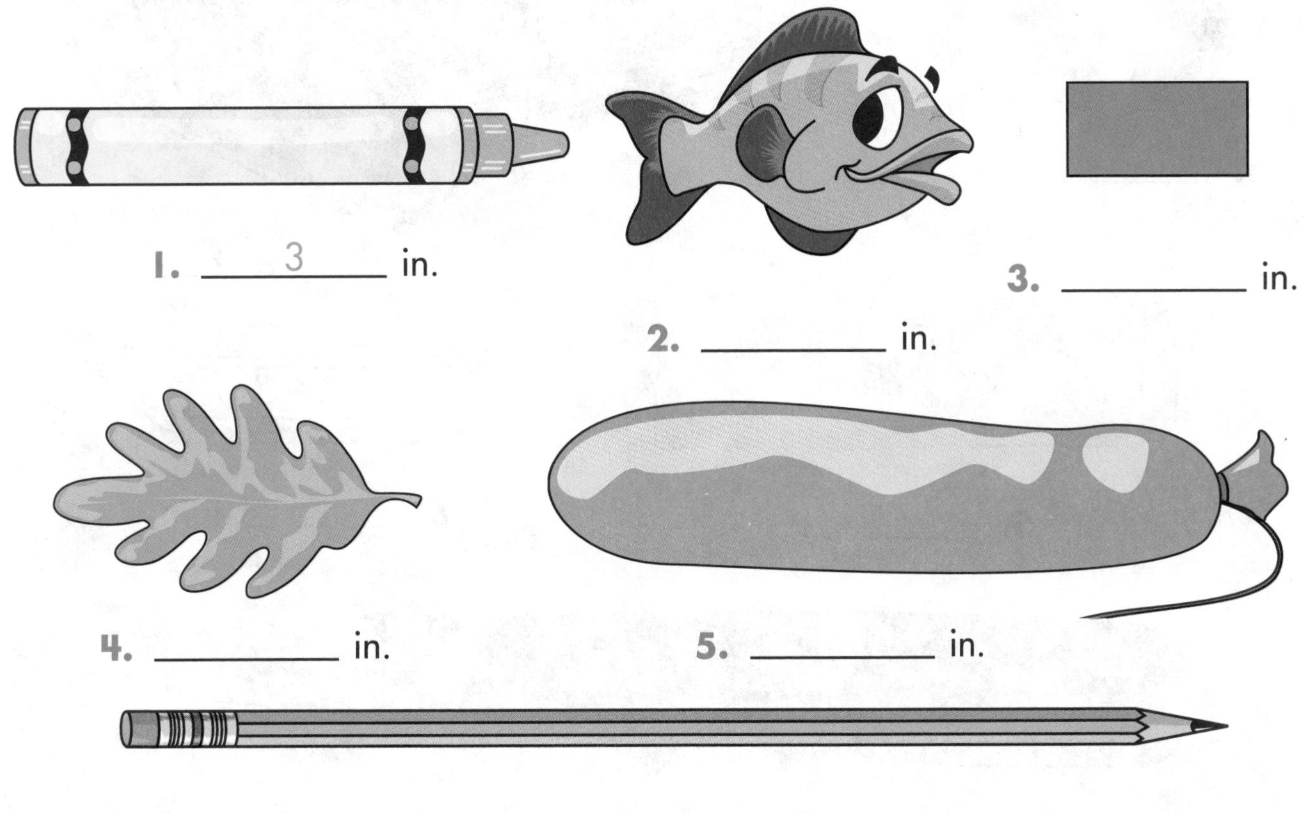

6. ______ in.

NAME ____________________

Lesson 8.1 Measuring in Inches

Use a ruler to find the length of each object to the nearest inch.

1. ___1___ in.

2.  ________ in.

3. ________ in.

4. ________ in.

5. ________ in.

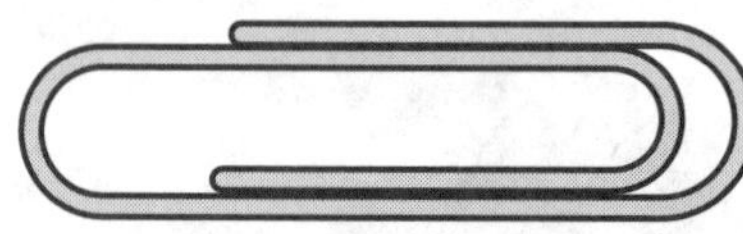

6. ________ in.

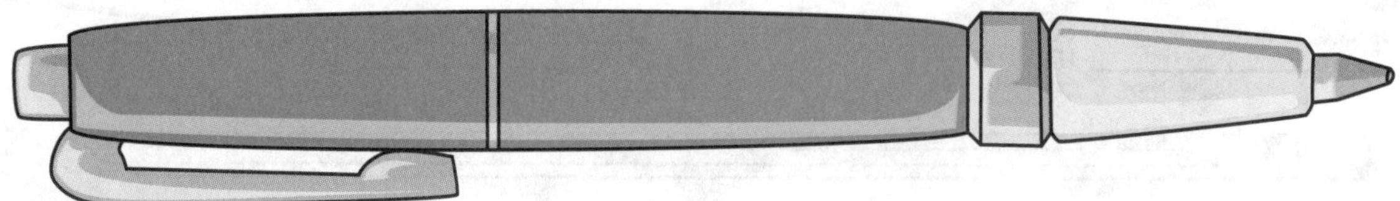

7. ________ in.

NAME ___________________________

Lesson 8.2 Converting Units of Length (inches, feet, and yards)

Conversion Table

1 foot (ft.) = 12 inches (in.)

1 yard (yd.) = 3 feet (ft.)

1 yard (yd.) = 36 inches (in.)

When converting from long to short, multiply.

2 ft. = _____ in.
Know: 1 ft. = 12 in.
$2 \times 12 = 24$
2 ft. = 24 in.

When converting from short to long, divide.

9 ft. = _____ yd.
Know: 3 ft. = 1 yd.
$9 \div 3 = 3$
9 ft. = 3 yd.

Complete the following.

	a	b	c
1.	3 ft. = 36 in.	24 in. = ______ ft.	4 yd. = ______ in.
2.	12 in. = ______ ft.	21 ft. = ______ yd.	2 yd. = ______ ft.
3.	36 in. = ______ yd.	5 yd. = ______ in.	6 yd. = ______ in.
4.	5 yd. = ______ ft.	36 in. = ______ ft.	4 yd. = ______ ft.
5.	1 ft. = ______ in.	3 yd. = ______ ft.	6 ft. = ______ yd.
6.	15 ft. = ______ yd.	9 yd. = ______ in.	3 yd. = ______ in.
7.	6 ft. = ______ yd.	27 ft. = ______ yd.	2 ft. = ______ in.
8.	6 ft. = ______ in.	5 ft. = ______ in.	8 yd. = ______ in.
9.	2 yd. = ______ in.	18 ft. = ______ yd.	9 ft. = ______ yd.
10.	12 ft. = ______ yd.	4 ft. = ______ in.	24 ft. = ______ yd.
11.	7 ft. = ______ in.	7 yd. = ______ in.	6 yd. = ______ ft.
12.	3 ft. = ______ yd.	7 yd. = ______ ft.	8 yd. = ______ ft.

NAME ____________________

Lesson 8.3 Measuring Liquid Volume (cups, pints, quarts, and gallons)

Conversion Table
1 pint (pt.) = 2 cups (c.)
1 quart (qt.) = 2 pints (pt.)
1 quart (qt.) = 4 cups (c.)
1 gallon (gal.) = 4 quarts (qt.)
1 gallon (gal.) = 8 pints (pt.)
1 gallon (gal.) = 16 cups (c.)

When converting from more to less, multiply.

7 qt. = ____ pt.
Know: 1 qt. = 2 pt.
$7 \times 2 = 14$
7 qt. = 14 pt.

When converting from less to more, divide.

16 qt. = ____ gal.
Know: 4 qt. = 1 gal.
$16 \div 4 = 4$
16 qt. = 4 gal.

Complete the following.

	a	b	c
1.	2 pt. = 4 c.	32 c. = ____ gal.	40 pt. = ____ gal.
2.	12 c. = ____ qt.	2 gal. = ____ qt.	32 c. = ____ qt.
3.	8 c. = ____ qt.	10 pt. = ____ c.	64 pt. = ____ gal.
4.	4 qt. = ____ c.	3 qt. = ____ pt.	2 c. = ____ pt.
5.	16 c. = ____ gal.	10 pt. = ____ qt.	8 c. = ____ pt.
6.	2 gal. = ____ pt.	16 c. = ____ qt.	5 qt. = ____ c.
7.	5 gal. = ____ qt.	24 qt. = ____ gal.	6 pt. = ____ c.
8.	20 qt. = ____ gal.	14 pt. = ____ qt.	3 gal. = ____ qt.
9.	17 qt. = ____ pt.	32 pt. = ____ gal.	9 gal. = ____ c.
10.	5 gal. = ____ c.	10 c. = ____ pt.	8 qt. = ____ pt.
11.	3 gal. = ____ qt.	16 c. = ____ pt.	10 qt. = ____ c.
12.	16 pt. = ____ gal.	8 pt. = ____ qt.	13 pt. = ____ c.

NAME ______________________

Lesson 8.4 Measuring Weight (ounces and pounds)

Pounds and ounces measure weight.

1 pound (lb.) = 16 ounces (oz.)

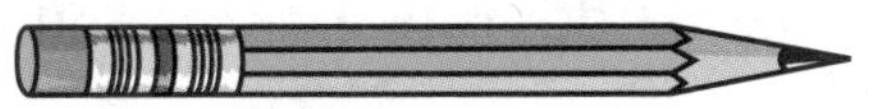

A pencil weighs about an ounce.

A can of peas weighs about a pound.

Use the example above to answer questions 1–6.

1. Which weighs more, an ounce or a pound? ________
2. Which weighs less, 18 ounces or 1 pound? ________
3. Which weighs more, 32 ounces of sugar or 2 pounds of sugar? ________
4. Which weighs less, 14 ounces of cheese or 2 pounds of cheese? ________
5. Would a toy car be more likely to weigh 5 ounces or 5 pounds? ________
6. Would a television be more likely to weigh 40 ounces or 40 pounds? ________

Tell whether you would use ounces or pounds to measure each of the following.

	a	b	c
7.	a feather ______	a plastic hanger ______	a pumpkin ______
8.	a pack of gum ______	a flower ______	an apricot ______
9.	a table ______	a bag of potting soil ______	a grasshopper ______
10.	a bucket of rocks ______	a baby ______	a turkey ______

NAME ______________________

Lesson 8.5 Temperature

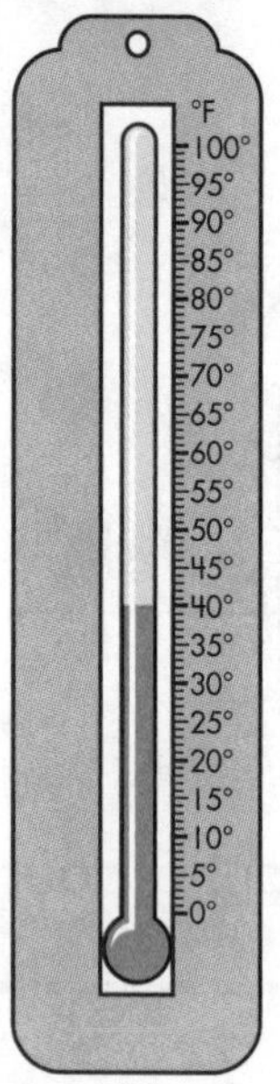

A thermometer measures the temperature in degrees Fahrenheit.

Water will freeze at 32 degrees Fahrenheit (32°F).

The temperature on this thermometer is 40 degrees Fahrenheit (40°F).

What is the temperature reading on each thermometer?

	a	b	c
1.	20 °F	___ °F	___ °F
2.	___ °F	___ °F	___ °F
3.	___ °F	___ °F	___ °F

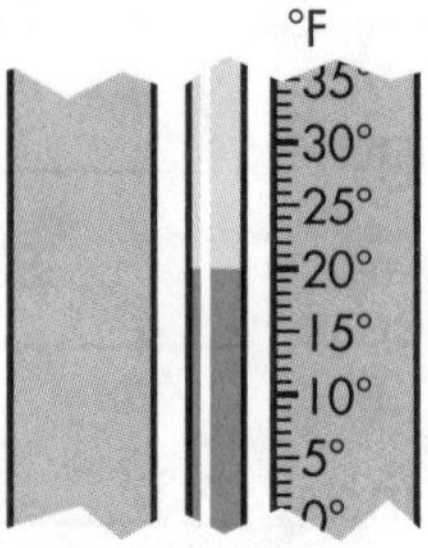

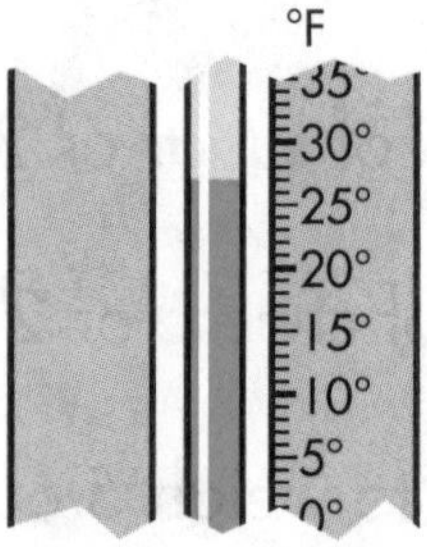

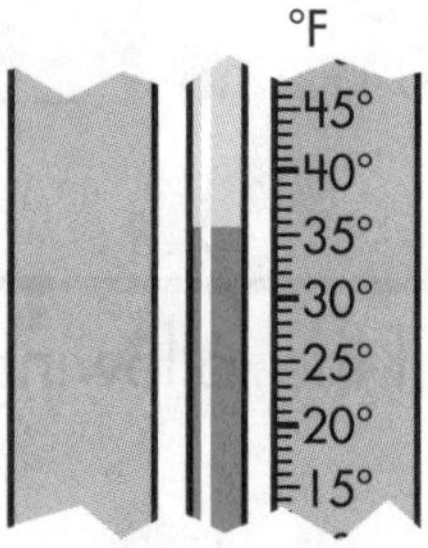

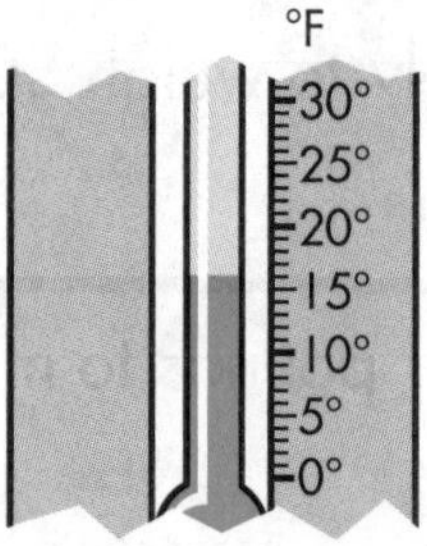

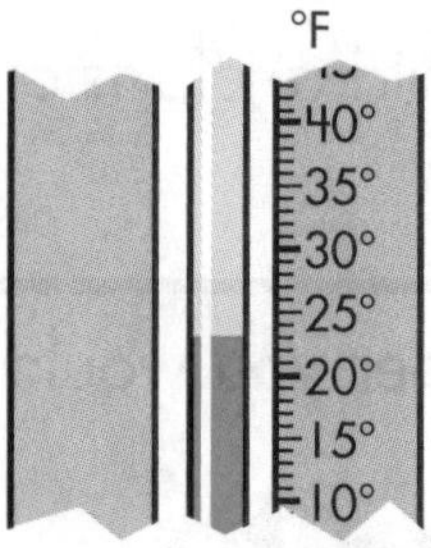

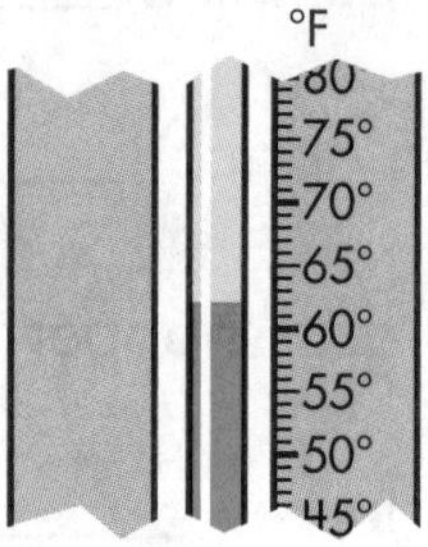

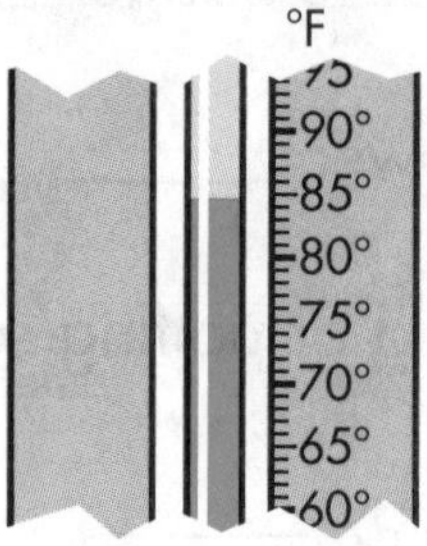

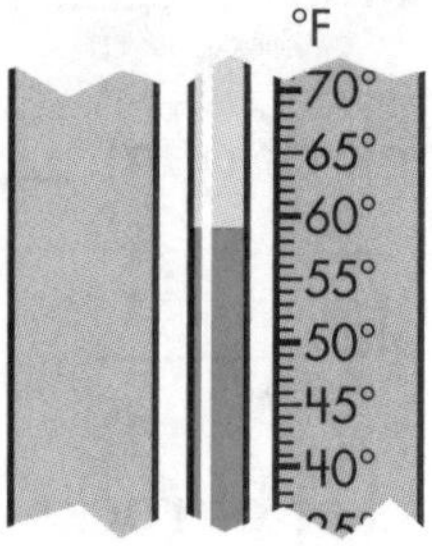

NAME ______________________

Lesson 8.6 Problem Solving

SHOW YOUR WORK

Solve each problem.

1. Danny caught a fish that was 2 feet long. How long was the fish in inches?

   The fish was ________ inches long.

2. Ashley is 48 inches tall. How tall is she in feet?

   Ashley is ________ feet tall.

3. A recipe calls for 4 cups of water. How many pints of water is the recipe calling for?

   The recipe is calling for ________ pints of water.

4. Jim had 2 gallons of paint. He used 6 quarts. How many quarts does he have left?

   Jim has ________ quarts left.

5. Would you measure the water in a swimming pool in cups, pints, quarts, or gallons?

   You would measure the water in a swimming pool in ________.

6. Would you measure the juice in a glass in cups, pints, quarts, or gallons?

   You would measure the juice in ________.

7. The thermometer reads 34° Fahrenheit. Is this measurement considered hot or cold?

   This measurement is considered ________.

8. The thermometer reads 89° Fahrenheit. Is this measurement considered hot or cold?

   This measurement is considered ________.

1.	2.
3.	4.
5.	6.
7.	8.

NAME ______________________

Lesson 8.7 Problem Solving

SHOW YOUR WORK

Solve each problem.

1. Hiroshi is 3 feet 10 inches tall. His brother, Akira, is 48 inches tall. Who is taller?

   Hiroshi is __________ inches tall.

   Akira is __________ inches tall.

   __________ is taller.

2. A table is 2 yards in length. How long is it in feet?

   The table is __________ feet long.

3. Would you measure a toy car in inches, feet, or yards?

   You would measure a toy car in __________.

4. Would you measure the length of a football field in inches, feet, or yards?

   You would measure a football field in __________.

5. Inez weighed 6 pounds at birth. How many ounces did she weigh at birth?

   Inez weighed __________ ounces at birth.

6. Would you measure a dog in ounces or pounds?

   You would measure a dog in __________.

7. The thermometer read 63° Fahrenheit. How many degrees is this above the temperature at which water freezes?

   The thermometer reads __________ °F.

   Water freezes at __________ °F.

   It is __________ °F above freezing.

1.	
2.	3.
4.	5.
6.	7.

NAME ____________

Check What You Learned

Customary Measurement

Use a ruler to find the length of each object to the nearest inch.

1. ________ in.

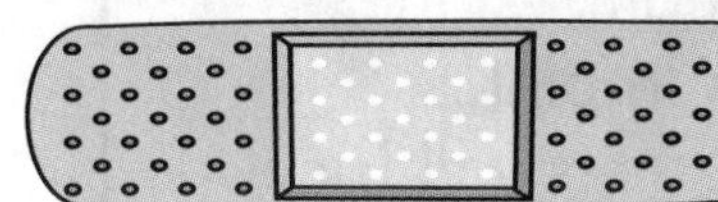

2. ________ in.

3. ________ in.

CHAPTER 8 POSTTEST

SHOW YOUR WORK

Solve each problem.

4. Ruth needs 5 yards of fabric. How many feet of fabric does Ruth need?

   Ruth needs _____ feet of fabric.

5. A truck has a height of 8 feet 11 inches. It needs to go under a bridge that has a clearance of 96 inches. Can the truck go under this bridge?

   The truck ________ go under this bridge.

6. At the age of 5, Tom was 3 feet 4 inches tall. When he was 8 years old he was 4 feet tall. How many inches did Tom grow?

   Tom grew _____ inches.

7. A recipe calls for 5 quarts of water. How many cups of water does it call for?

   The recipe calls for _____ cups of water.

8. Mr. Armas drank 16 cups of coffee in one week. How many gallons of coffee did Mr. Armas drink in 1 week?

   Mr. Armas drank _____ gallon(s) of coffee in 1 week.

4.	
5.	
6.	
7.	8.

NAME ____________________

Check What You Learned

SHOW YOUR WORK

Customary Measurement

Solve each problem.

9. Which weighs more, a 30-ounce bag of fruit or a 3-pound bag of vegetables?

The __________ weigh(s) more.

10. Lucy wants to buy 5 quarts of cream. At the grocery store, cream only comes in pint containers. How many pint containers will Lucy need to buy to equal 5 quarts of cream?

Lucy will need to buy _____ pint containers to equal five quarts of cream.

11. Would a chair be more likely to weigh 5 ounces or 5 pounds?

A chair would more likely weigh __________.

12. Would you be more likely to measure the length of a swimming pool in inches or yards?

You would measure a swimming pool in _______.

13. Would you be more likely to measure the height of an adult in inches or feet?

You would measure an adult in __________.

14. Would you measure the amount of water in a glass in cups, pints, or quarts?

You would measure the water in a glass in _____.

15. Today, the thermometer reads 86° Fahrenheit. How many degrees is that above the point at which water freezes?

It is _____ °F above freezing.

9.	10.
11.	12.
13.	14.
15.	

NAME ____________________

Check What You Know

Metric Measurement

Use a ruler to find the length of each object to the nearest centimeter.

1. ____________ cm 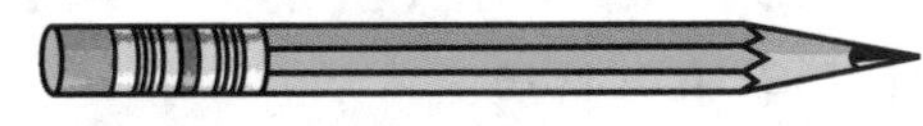

2. ____________ cm

3. ____________ cm 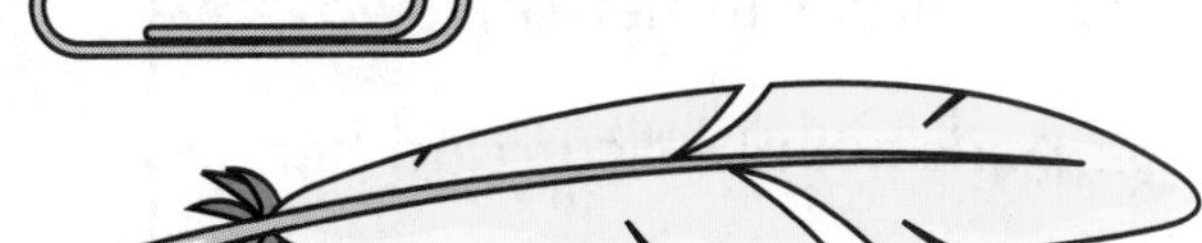

Complete the following.

	a	b	c
4.	2 m = _____ cm	5,000 g = _____ kg	8,000 mL = _____ L
5.	5,000 mg = _____ g	1 L = _____ mL	5 m = _____ cm
6.	5 L = _____ mL	7 kg = _____ g	7 g = _____ mg
7.	300 cm = _____ m	3 m = _____ cm	4,000 mL = _____ L
8.	5 kg = _____ g	2 g = _____ mg	200 cm = _____ m
9.	4 m = _____ cm	6,000 mg = _____ g	6 m = _____ cm

What is the temperature reading on each thermometer?

10.

a

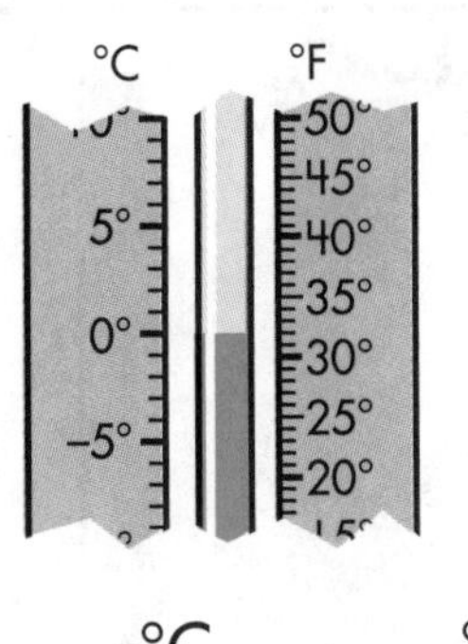

_____ °C _____ °F

b

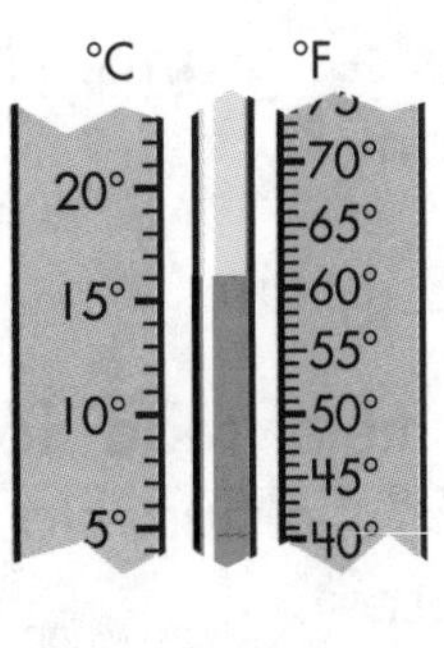

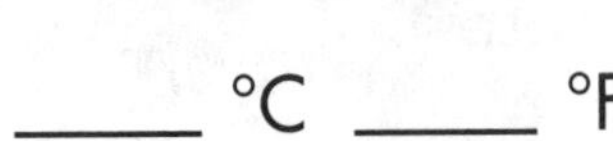

_____ °C _____ °F

c

°C °F 25° 20° 15° 85° 80° 75° 70° 65° 60° 55°

_____ °C _____ °F

NAME ____________________

Check What You Know

Metric Measurement

SHOW YOUR WORK

Solve each problem.

11. Mrs. Chen's driveway is 6 meters long. Her car is 2 meters 23 centimeters long. Her truck is 3 meters 95 centimeters long. Can Mrs. Chen park both her car and her truck in her driveway?

Mrs. Chen ________ park both her car and her truck in her driveway.

12. Tina is 1 meter 44 centimeters tall. Shawn is 124 centimeters tall. Who is taller?

________ is taller.

13. A carton contains 2 liters of juice. If 1,300 milliliters are used, how many milliliters are left?

There are ________ milliliters of juice left.

14. A 1-liter container has 5 servings in it. How many milliliters is each serving?

Each serving is ________ milliliters.

15. The saltshaker holds 5 grams of salt. If a grain of salt weighs 1 milligram, how many grains of salt are in the saltshaker?

There are ________ grains of salt in the saltshaker.

16. A plant weighs 6 kilograms 57 grams. How much does the plant weigh in grams?

The plant weighs ________ grams.

17. In the morning, the thermometer read 46° Celsius. In the afternoon, it read 34° Celsius. How much did the temperature decrease?

The temperature decreased ________°C.

11.	
12.	13.
14.	15.
16.	17.

NAME ______________________

Lesson 9.1 Measuring in Centimeters

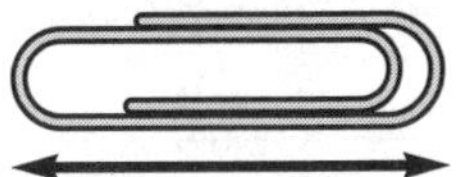

The paper clip is 3 centimeters or 3 cm long.

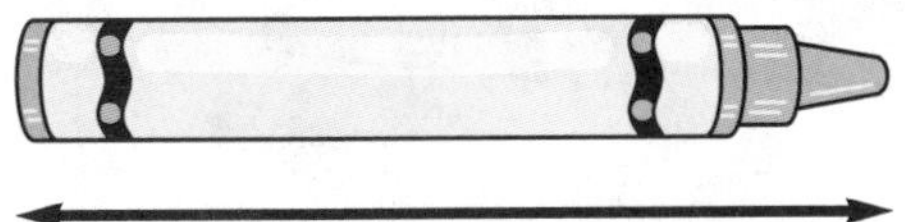

The crayon is 6 cm long.

Use a ruler to find the length of each object to the nearest centimeter.

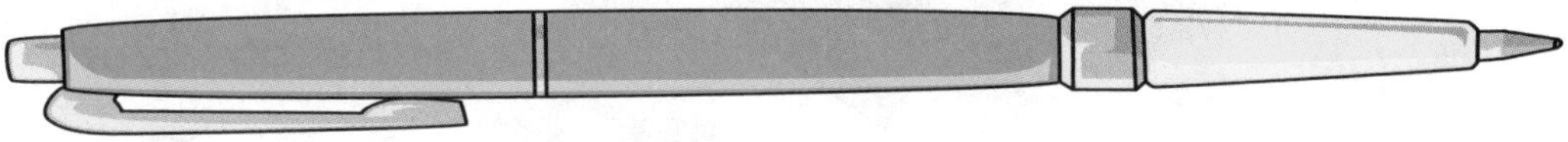

1. __14__ cm

2. ______ cm

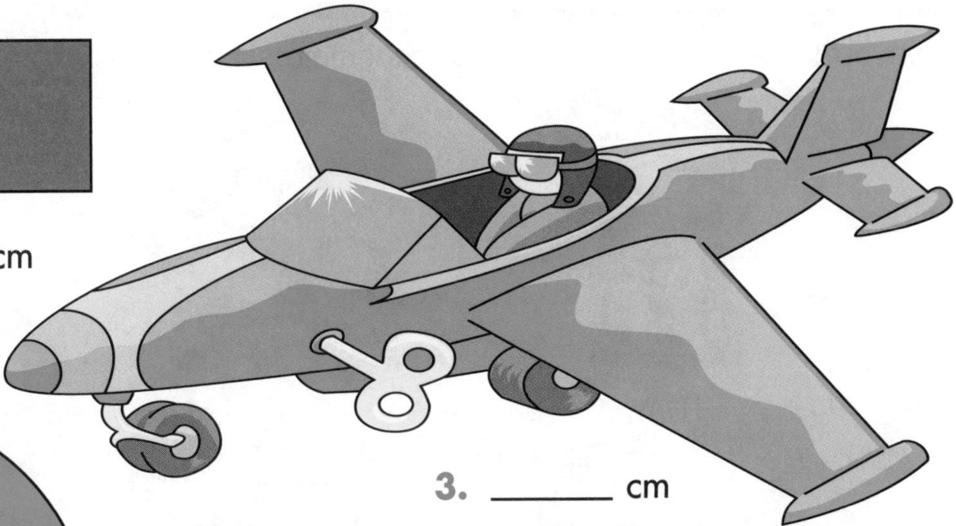

3. ______ cm

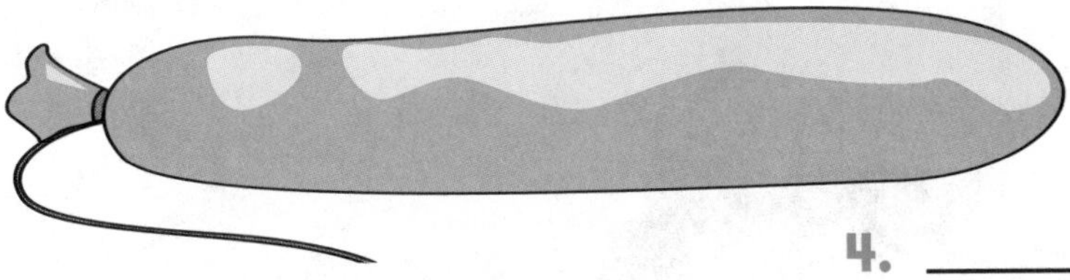

4. ______ cm

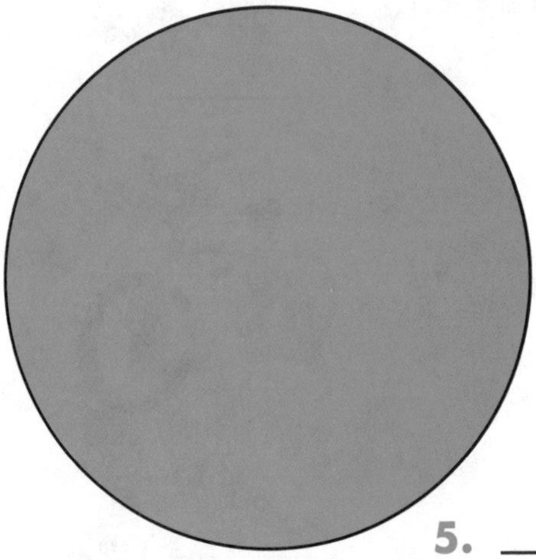

5. ______ cm

6. ______ cm

NAME ____________________

Lesson 9.1 Measuring in Centimeters

Use a ruler to find the length of each object to the nearest centimeter.

1. ___6___ cm

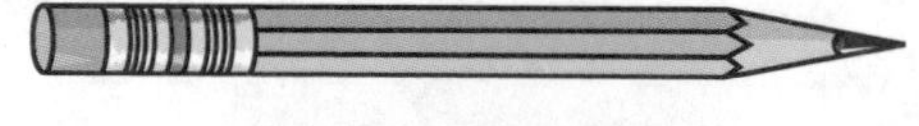

2. ________ cm

3. ________ cm

1 meter (m) = 100 centimeters (cm)

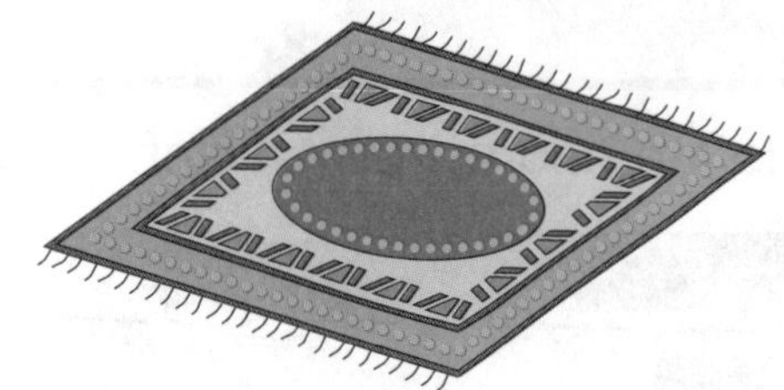

This rug is 200 cm long.

How long is it in meters?

The rug is 2 m long.

Convert these lengths to meters or centimeters.

	a	b	c

4.	10 m	200 cm	600 cm
	___1,000___ cm	______ m	______ m

5.	12 m	3 m	2 m
	______ cm	______ cm	______ cm

NAME ______________________

Lesson 9.2 Measuring Liquid Volume (liters)

A liter (L) is used to measure liquid volume.

A single serving of fruit juice is usually sold by the liter.

1 liter (L) = 1,000 milliliters (mL)

Complete the following.

	a	b	c
1.	3 L = 3,000 mL	2 L = ________ mL	7,000 mL = ________ L
2.	2,000 mL = ________ L	4,000 mL = ________ L	5 L = ________ mL

Answer the following questions.

3. Which is less, 500 milliliters or 5 liters? ________
4. Which is more, 4,534 milliliters or 4 liters? ________
5. Would the water in a wading pool be more likely to be 500 liters or 500 milliliters? ________
6. Would a glass of juice be more likely to be 300 milliliters or 300 liters? ________

Write whether you would use milliliters or liters to measure each of the following.

	a	b	c
7.	a bucket of water liters	a bottle of liquid soap ________	a bottle of perfume ________
8.	a bottle of lotion ________	a watering can full of water ________	a pitcher of lemonade ________

NAME ____________________

Lesson 9.3 Measuring Weight (grams and kilograms)

Conversion Table
1 gram (g) = 1,000 milligrams (mg)
1 kilogram (kg) = 1,000 grams (g)

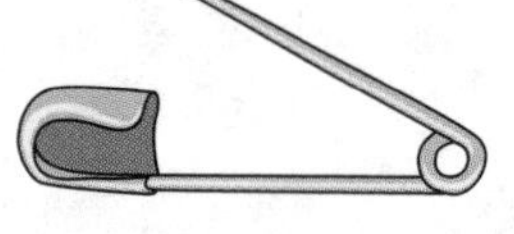

A grain of sand weighs about 1 mg.

A safety pin weighs about 1 g.

A jar of peanut butter weighs about 1 kg.

Use the information above to answer questions 1–4.

1. Which weighs more, a gram or a milligram? __________
2. Which weighs less, a gram or a kilogram? __________
3. How many safety pins would weigh the same as one jar of peanut butter? __________
4. 3,000 grains of sand would equal how many safety pins? __________

Write whether you would use milligrams (mg), grams (g), or kilograms (kg) to measure each of the following.

	a	b	c
5.	a baby kilograms	a grain of salt __________	a brick __________
6.	a couch __________	a raindrop __________	an ice cube __________
7.	a paper clip __________	a sugar cube __________	an umbrella __________
8.	a feather __________	a pencil __________	a shoe __________

Lesson 9.4 Temperature

A thermometer can measure the temperature in degrees Fahrenheit (°F) and in degrees Celsius (°C).

Water freezes at 0 degrees Celsius (0°C).

Water freezes at 32 degrees Fahrenheit (32°F).

The temperature on this thermometer is 20 degrees Celsius (20°C). It is also at 68°F. 20°C is equivalent to 68°F.

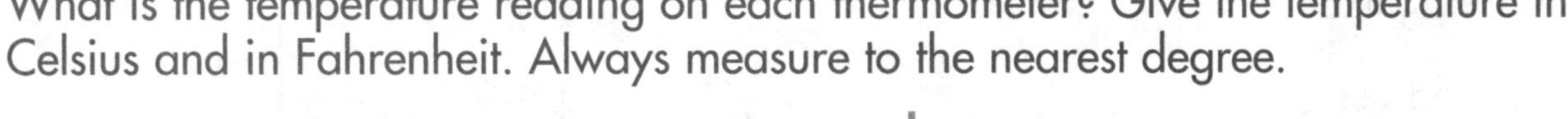

What is the temperature reading on each thermometer? Give the temperature in Celsius and in Fahrenheit. Always measure to the nearest degree.

a b c

1.

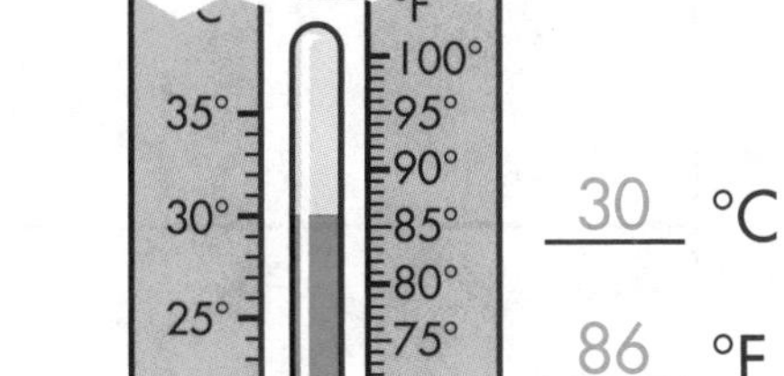

30 °C
86 °F

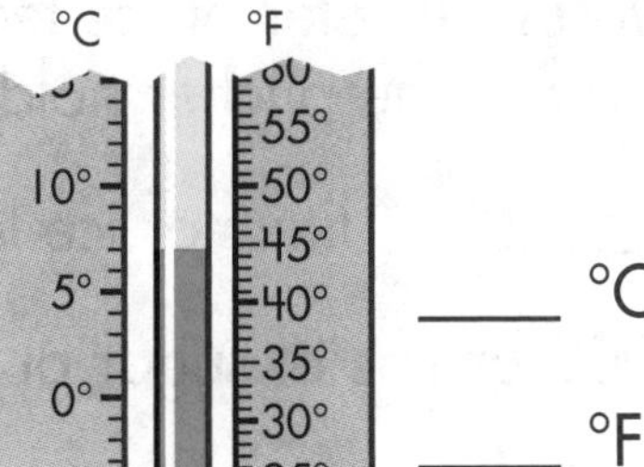

____ °C
____ °F

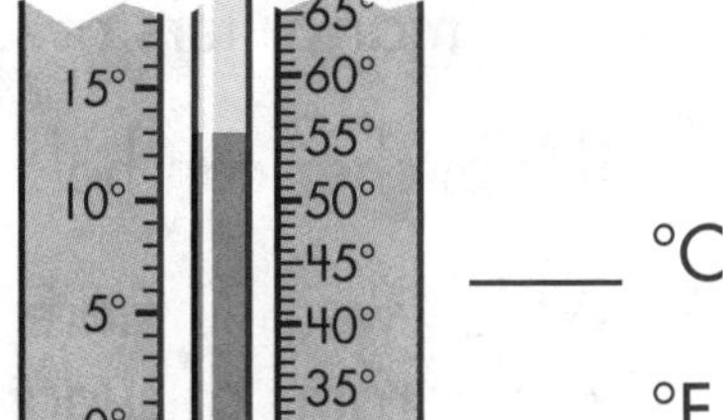

____ °C
____ °F

2.

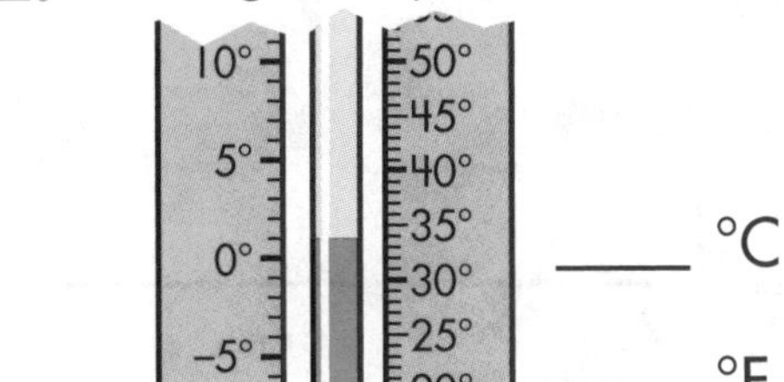

____ °C
____ °F

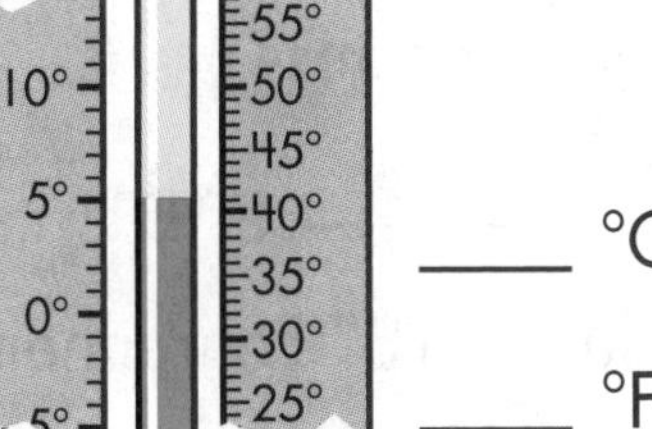

____ °C
____ °F

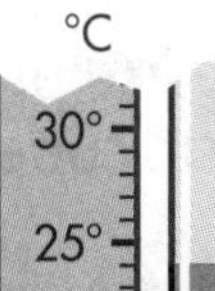

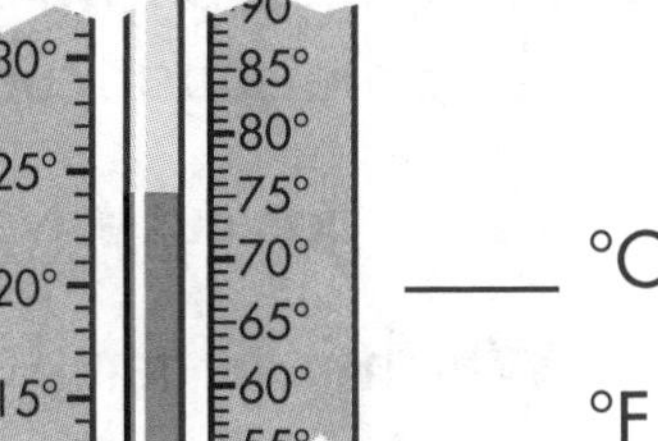

____ °C
____ °F

3.

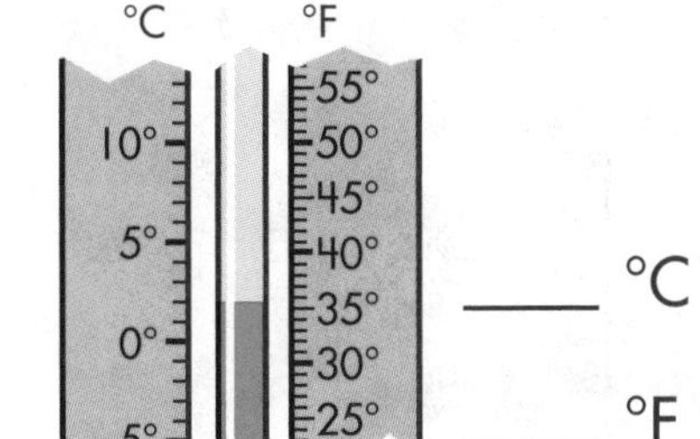

____ °C
____ °F

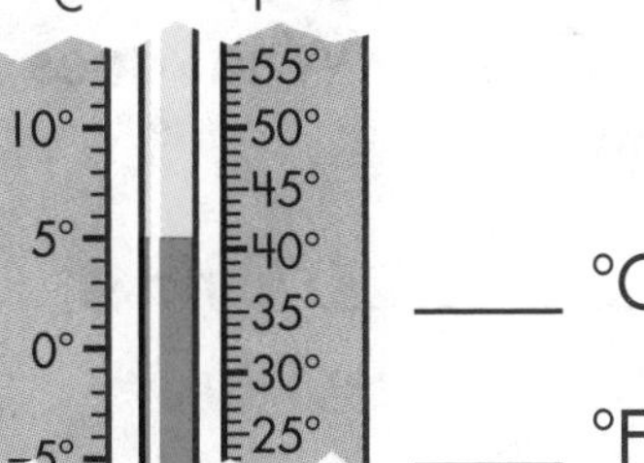

____ °C
____ °F

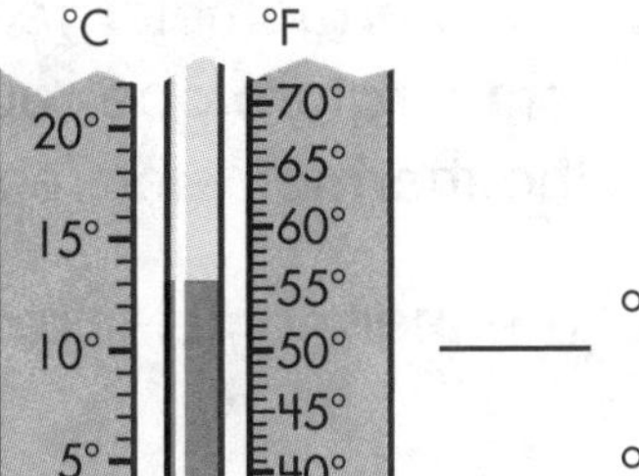

____ °C
____ °F

NAME ______________________

Lesson 9.5 Problem Solving

SHOW YOUR WORK

Solve each problem.

1. A pencil is 10 centimeters long. How many pencils laid end–to–end would it take to equal 1 meter?

   It would take __________ pencils.

2. A couch measured 2 meters in length. How many centimeters in length is it?

   It is __________ centimeter in length.

3. Would you use liters or milliliters to measure a glass of tomato juice?

   You would use __________.

4. The pitcher can hold 3,000 millimeter of ice tea. How many liters of ice tea can the pitcher hold?

   The pitcher can hold __________ liters of ice tea.

5. Which weighs more, 1,000 grams of sugar or 2 kilograms of sugar?

   The __________ of sugar weighs more.

6. A sugar cube weighs 2,000 milligrams. How much does the sugar cube weigh in grams?

   The sugar cube weighs __________ grams.

7. Which is hotter, 10° Celsius or 10° Fahrenheit?

   __________ is hotter.

8. The thermometer reads 13° Celsius. The temperature goes up 10° Celsius. What does the thermometer read now?

   The thermometer reads__________°C now.

1.	2.
3.	4.
5.	6.
7.	8.

NAME ____________________

Check What You Learned

Metric Measurement

CHAPTER 9 POSTTEST

Use a ruler to find the length of each object to the nearest centimeter.

2. ________ cm

1. ________ cm

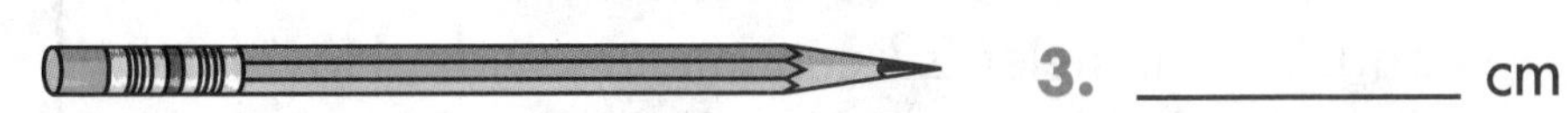

3. ________ cm

Complete the following.

	a	b	c
4.	300 cm = _____ m	5,000 mg = _____ g	400 cm = _____ m
5.	200 cm = _____ m	5 m = _____ cm	6 m = _____ cm
6.	3 g = _____ mg	8,000 g = _____ kg	5,000 mL = _____ L
7.	6,000 mL = _____ L	3,000 g = _____ kg	7 m = _____ cm
8.	7,000 mg = _____ g	4,000 mL = _____ L	2,000 mL = _____ L
9.	5 L = _____ mL	7 g = _____ mg	8 kg = _____ g

What is the temperature reading on each thermometer?

10.

a

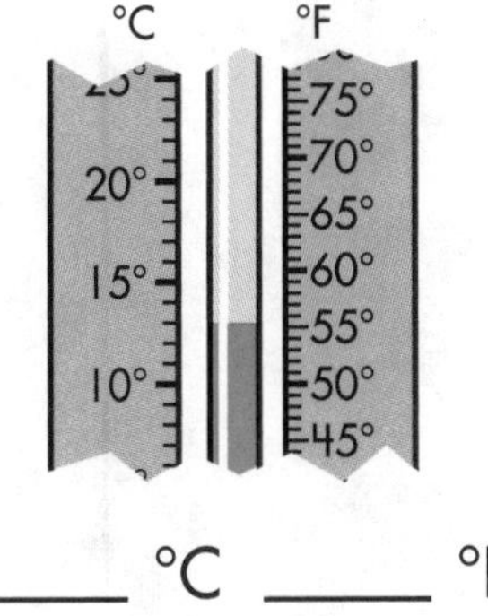

_____ °C _____ °F

b

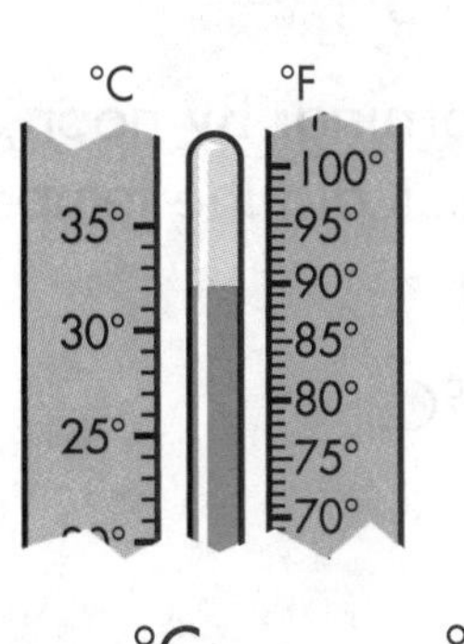

_____ °C _____ °F

c

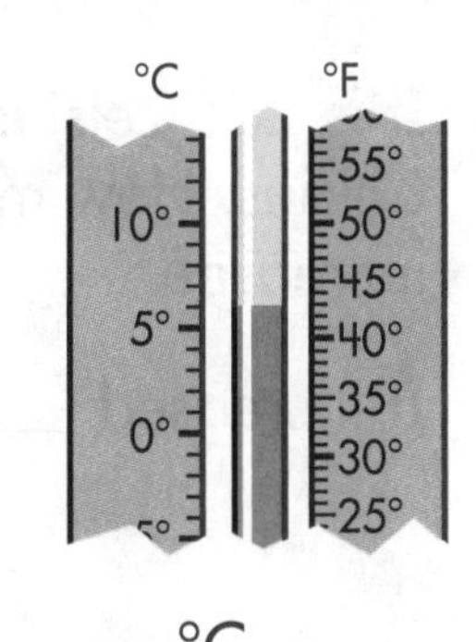

_____ °C _____ °F

NAME ____________________

Check What You Learned

Metric Measurement

SHOW YOUR WORK

Solve each problem.

11. Suni is 1 meter 3 centimeters tall. How tall is Suni in centimeters?

Suni is __________ centimeters tall.

12. Mr. Thomas's garden is 2 meters 15 centimeters long. It is 1 meter 23 centimeters wide. How long and wide is his garden in centimeters?

The garden is __________ centimeters long and __________ centimeters wide.

13. Christopher has 1 liter of milk. He uses 300 milliliters of the milk in a recipe. How many milliliters of milk does he have left?

Christopher has __________ milliliters of milk left.

14. A teakettle can hold 2 liters of water. How many milliliters does the teakettle hold?

The teakettle holds __________ milliliters of water.

15. Alice weighs 95 kilograms. How many grams does she weigh?

Alice weighs __________ grams.

16. It is 23° Celsius in the morning. By noon, it is 46° Celsius. How many degrees did the temperature increase?

It increased __________°C.

11.	12.
13.	14.
15.	16.

NAME ______________________

Check What You Know

Money, Time, and Calendar

Complete the following.

1. 30 pennies have a value of ________ cents or ________ nickels.
2. 50 pennies have a value of ________ cents or ________ half dollar.
3. $3.23 means ________ dollars and ________ cents.
4. $10.09 means ________ dollars and ________ cents.

Add or subtract.

	a	b	c	d	e
5.	$ 3.06 .45 + 13.92	$23.57 − 16.43	62¢ +19¢	96¢ −43¢	$ 6.45 13.96 + 22.42

Write the value of each collection.

6.

a

____

b

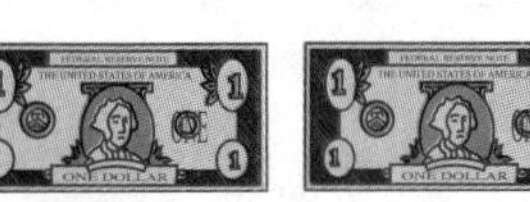

____

Compare the two sets of collections. Use "greater than," "less than," or "equal to."

7.

____

____

________ is ________ ________.

NAME ____________________

Check What You Know

Money, Time, and Calendar

Determine the change for the following.

8. A yoyo costs $3.53.

money value $ ________
cost of yoyo − ________
change $ ________

Complete the following.

	a	b
9.	2:32 means ___ minutes after ___.	2:32 means ___ minutes to ___.
10.	3:45 means ___ minutes after ___.	3:45 means ___ minutes to ___.
11.	7:06 means ___ minutes after ___.	9:50 means ___ minutes to ___.

Tell the time to the nearest hour, half hour, quarter hour, or minute as indicated.

12.

a	b	c	d
hour	half hour	quarter hour	minute
___ : ___	___ : ___	___ : ___	___ : ___

Complete the following.

	a	b	c
13.	There are _____ days in a year.	There are _____ months in a year.	There are _____ days in a week.
14.	There are _____ hours in a day.	There are _____ minutes in an hour.	February _____ occurs only in leap years.
15.	2 hours 3 minutes _____ minutes	63 minutes _____ hour 3 minutes	1 day 2 hours _____ hours

NAME ______________________

Lesson 10.1 Money: Using Decimals

1 penny	1 nickel	1 dime	1 quarter	1 half dollar	1 dollar
1 cent	5 cents	10 cents	25 cents	50 cents	100 cents
1¢	5¢	10¢	25¢	50¢	100¢
or	or	or	or	or	or
$0.01	$0.05	$0.10	$0.25	$0.50	$1.00

10 pennies have a value of __10__ cents or __1__ dime.

15 pennies have a value of __15__ cents or __3__ nickels.

$5.52 means __5__ dollars and __52__ cents.

$7.03 means __7__ dollars and __3__ cents.

Complete the following.

1. 20 pennies have a value of _____ cents or _____ dimes.
2. 50 pennies have a value of _____ cents or _____ quarters.
3. 2 quarters have a value of _____ cents or _____ half dollar.
4. 10 dimes have a value of _____ cents or _____ dollar.
5. 5 nickels have a value of _____ cents or _____ quarter.
6. 30 pennies have a value of _____ cents or _____ dimes.
7. $17.43 means _____ dollars and _____ cents.
8. $16.07 means _____ dollars and _____ cents.
9. $5.95 means _____ dollars and _____ cents.
10. $3.23 means _____ dollars and _____ cents.
11. $12.50 means _____ dollars and _____ cents.
12. $9.17 means _____ dollars and _____ cents.

NAME ____________________

Lesson 10.2 Money: Adding and Subtracting with Decimals

Be sure to line up the decimal points.

Add or subtract as usual.

Put a decimal point (.) and a $ or ¢ in the answer.

$10.03	45¢	$9.87	76¢
+ .96	+22¢	− 6.52	−29¢
$10.99	67¢	$3.35	47¢

Add or subtract.

	a	b	c	d	e
1.	$2.03 + 5.97 $8.00	$13.56 + 1.72	$56.96 + 5.42	$7.52 + 3.85	$40.30 + .47
2.	$ 3.59 22.19 + 6.70	$4.36 3.52 + .46	$22.59 13.21 + 5.50	46¢ 13¢ +30¢	$13.57 20.92 + 4.16
3.	$25.36 − 1.24	$56.43 − 33.29	$96.00 − 17.00	$9.20 − .86	54¢ −23¢
4.	73¢ −69¢	$72.83 − 13.72	$54.00 − 30.00	$19.23 − 8.17	$4.05 − .44
5.	63¢ +19¢	93¢ −56¢	$13.93 + 7.21	$24.36 − 13.93	$45.23 − 19.00
6.	$5.43 − .92	$7.92 + 1.09	54¢ +29¢	93¢ −58¢	$59.92 − 7.80

NAME ____________________

Lesson 10.3 Counting Money

 $5.00

 $1.00

 50¢ or $0.50

 25¢ or $0.25

 10¢ or $0.10

 5¢ or $0.05

 1¢ or $0.01

$$\begin{array}{r} \$2.00 \\ .50 \\ +\ .03 \\ \hline \$2.53 \end{array}$$

2 dollars and 53 cents is $2.53.

Write the value of each collection.

	a		b	
1.	 	82¢		________
2.		________		________
3.		________		________

NAME ______________________

Lesson 10.3 Counting Money

58¢

63¢

58¢ is less than 63¢.

Compare the two sets of collections. Use "greater than," "less than," or "equal to."

1.  50¢ |  50¢

50¢ is equal to 50¢.

2.  ________ |  ________

________ is ________ ________.

3. ________ | ________

________ is ________ ________.

4.  ________ |  ________

________ is ________ ________.

NAME ____________________

Lesson 10.4 Making Change

A candy bar costs 79¢.

money value	$ 1.3 2
cost of candy bar	– .7 9
change	$ 0.5 3

Determine the change for the following.

1. A book costs $4.34.

money value	$ 6.50
cost of book	– 4.34
change	$ 2.16

2. A calculator costs $6.82.

money value	$ ______
cost of calculator	– ______
change	$ ______

3. A pack of gum costs $1.23.

money value	$ ______
cost of gum	– ______
change	$ ______

4. A dictionary costs $3.46.

money value	$ ______
cost of dictionary	– ______
change	$ ______

5. A roll of film costs $2.57.

money value	$ ______
cost of film	– ______
change	$ ______

NAME ____________________________

Lesson 10.5 Telling Time

5:15 is read "five fifteen" and means "15 minutes after 5."

12:50 is read "twelve fifty" and means "50 minutes after 12" or "10 minutes to 1."

4:45 is read "four forty-five" and means "45 minutes after 5" or "15 minutes to 6."

Complete the following.

	a	b
1.	6:15 means <u>15</u> minutes after <u>6</u>.	11:50 means ____ minutes to ____.
2.	7:50 means ____ minutes after ____.	7:50 means ____ minutes to ____.
3.	12:45 means ____ minutes after ____.	12:45 means ____ minutes to ____.
4.	1:30 means ____ minutes after ____.	1:30 means ____ minutes to ____.

For each analog clock face, write the numerals that name the time.

	a	b	c	d
5.	 ____ : ____	 ____ : ____	 ____ : ____	 ____ : ____
6.	 ____ : ____	 ____ : ____	 ____ : ____	____ : ____

NAME ______________________

Lesson 10.5 Telling Time

6:41

The closest hour on an analog clock is determined by the hour hand (the short hand).

The closest half hour, quarter hour, and minute are determined by the minute hand (the long hand).

A half hour is at 30 minutes or 1 hour.

A quarter hour is at 15, 30, 45 minutes, or 1 hour.

What time is it to the nearest hour? __7:00__, half hour? __6:30__, quarter hour? __6:45__, minute? __6:41__

Write the time to the nearest hour, half hour, quarter hour, or minute as indicated.

	a	b	c	d
1.	hour ___ : ___	half hour ___ : ___	quarter hour ___ : ___	minute ___ : ___
2.	hour ___ : ___	half hour ___ : ___	quarter hour ___ : ___	minute ___ : ___

Draw the hands on the analog clock to express the time presented on the digital clock.

a

3.

b

4. 12:07

NAME ____________________

Lesson 10.6 Calendar

January

S	M	T	W	T	F	S
			1	2	3	4
5	6	7	8	9	10	11
12	13	14	15	16	17	18
19	20	21	22	23	24	25
26	27	28	29	30	31	

February

S	M	T	W	T	F	S
						1
2	3	4	5	6	7	8
9	10	11	12	13	14	15
16	17	18	19	20	21	22
23	24	25	26	27	28	

March

S	M	T	W	T	F	S
						1
2	3	4	5	6	7	8
9	10	11	12	13	14	15
16	17	18	19	20	21	22
23	24	25	26	27	28	29
30	31					

April

S	M	T	W	T	F	S
		1	2	3	4	5
6	7	8	9	10	11	12
13	14	15	16	17	18	19
20	21	22	23	24	25	26
27	28	29	30			

May

S	M	T	W	T	F	S
				1	2	3
4	5	6	7	8	9	10
11	12	13	14	15	16	17
18	19	20	21	22	23	24
25	26	27	28	29	30	31

June

S	M	T	W	T	F	S
1	2	3	4	5	6	7
8	9	10	11	12	13	14
15	16	17	18	19	20	21
22	23	24	25	26	27	28
29	30					

July

S	M	T	W	T	F	S
		1	2	3	4	5
6	7	8	9	10	11	12
13	14	15	16	17	18	19
20	21	22	23	24	25	26
27	28	29	30	31		

August

S	M	T	W	T	F	S
					1	2
3	4	5	6	7	8	9
10	11	12	13	14	15	16
17	18	19	20	21	22	23
24	25	26	27	28	29	30
31						

September

S	M	T	W	T	F	S
	1	2	3	4	5	6
7	8	9	10	11	12	13
14	15	16	17	18	19	20
21	22	23	24	25	26	27
28	29	30				

October

S	M	T	W	T	F	S
			1	2	3	4
5	6	7	8	9	10	11
12	13	14	15	16	17	18
19	20	21	22	23	24	25
26	27	28	29	30	31	

November

S	M	T	W	T	F	S
						1
2	3	4	5	6	7	8
9	10	11	12	13	14	15
16	17	18	19	20	21	22
23	24	25	26	27	28	29
30						

December

S	M	T	W	T	F	S
	1	2	3	4	5	6
7	8	9	10	11	12	13
14	15	16	17	18	19	20
21	22	23	24	25	26	27
28	29	30	31			

There are $365\frac{1}{4}$ days in a year. A leap year occurs every four years. In a **leap year,** February 29 is added to combine the $\frac{1}{4}$ days into 1 day. In a leap year calendar, there are 366 days. In all other calendar years there are 365 days.

Answer each question. Use the calendar to help you.

	a		b	
1.	How many months are in a year?	_____	How many months have 31 days?	_____
2.	How many days are in December?	_____	How many days are in February?	_____
3.	How many days are in February during a leap year?	_____	How many months have exactly 30 days?	_____
4.	How many days are in a week?	_____	How many full weeks are in May?	_____
5.	On what day is August 2?	_____	How many Mondays are in January?	_____
6.	What date falls 23 days before June 2?	_____	What date falls 16 days after September 29?	_____

There are 60 minutes in an hour. There are 24 hours in a day. Complete the following.

	a	b	c	d
7.	2 hours 15 minutes	1 hour 50 minutes	120 minutes	180 minutes
	___ minutes	___ minutes	___ hours	___ hours
8.	1 day 2 hours	2 days 5 hours	29 hours	48 hours
	___ hours	___ hours	___ day(s) ___ hours	___ days

NAME ______________________

Check What You Learned

Money, Time, and Calendar

Complete the following.

1. 25 pennies have a value of ________ cents or ________ quarter.
2. 4 quarters have a value of ________ cents or ________ dollar.
3. $6.19 means ________ dollars and ________ cents.
4. $5.26 means ________ dollars and ________ cents.

CHAPTER 10 POSTTEST

Add or subtract.

	a	b	c	d	e
5.	$45.63 − 32.91	54¢ 31¢ + 5¢	$59.61 5.03 + .17	$92.59 − 12.13	83¢ −64¢

Write the value of each collection.

6.

a

____

b

____

Compare the two sets of collections. Use "greater than," "less than," or "equal to."

7.

____

____

________ is ________ ________.

NAME ______________________

Check What You Learned

Money, Time, and Calendar

Determine the change for the following.

8. A book costs $3.48.

money value $ ________

cost of book − ________

change $ ________

Complete the following.

	a	b
9.	4:15 means ___ minutes after ___.	7:45 means ___ minutes to ___.
10.	12:55 means ___ minutes after ___.	12:55 means ___ minutes to ___.
11.	3:23 means ___ minutes after ___.	6:40 means ___ minutes to ___.

Tell the time to the nearest hour, half hour, quarter hour, or minute as indicated.

12.

a	b	c	d
hour	half hour	quarter hour	minute
___ : ___	___ : ___	___ : ___	___ : ___

Complete the following.

	a	b	c
13.	There are _____ hours in a day.	There are _____ months in a year.	There are _____ days in a leap year.
14.	There are _____ minutes in an hour.	There are _____ days in a week.	There are _____ days in a non-leap year.
15.	1 hour 33 minutes _____ minutes	70 minutes _____ hour 10 minutes	2 days 1 hour _____ hours

CHAPTER 10 POSTTEST

NAME ______________________

Check What You Know

Graphs and Probability

Use the picture graph to answer each question.

Students' Favorite Fruit

Apple	● ● ● ● ● ●
Orange	● ● ● ● ◖
Banana	● ● ● ● ● ●
Grape	● ●
Strawberry	● ● ● ◖
Peach	● ● ● ● ●

Key: ● = 2 students

1. Which fruit did the fewest students choose as their favorite? ________

2. Which 2 fruits did the most students choose as their favorite? ________

3. Seven students chose which fruit as their favorite? ________

4. How many students chose peach as their favorite fruit? ________

5. How many students chose orange as their favorite fruit? ________

Use the bar graph to answer each question.

Students' Favorite Color

Number of Students: 0 1 2 3 4 5 6 7 8 9 10 11 12 13 14

Color: Black, White, Red, Yellow, Blue, Pink

6. How many students chose red as their favorite color? ________

7. How many students chose yellow as their favorite color? ________

8. Which color did the fewest students choose as their favorite? ________

9. Which color did the most students choose as their favorite? ________

10. What is the difference between the blue and the white choices? ________

11. Six students chose which colors as their favorite? ________

12. Nine students chose which color as their favorite color? ________

NAME ____________________

Check What You Know

Graphs and Probability

Use the line graph to answer each question.

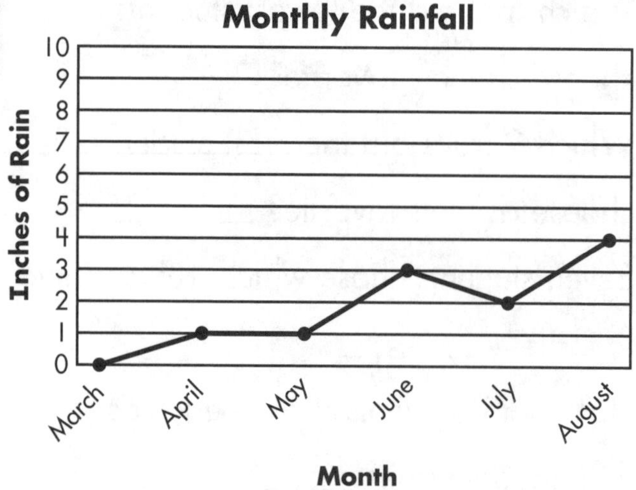

13. Which month had the most inches of rain? ________

14. Which month had the fewest inches of rain? ________

15. How many inches did it rain from March to August? ________

16. In which month did it rain 0 inches? ________

17. In which months did it rain 1 inch? ________________________

18. How many inches did it rain in June? ________ inches

19. How many inches did it rain in July? ________ inches

Write the correct probability for the following.

In a drawer you have 5 blue socks and 3 green socks.

20. What is the probability of pulling out a blue sock? ______

21. What is the probability of pulling out a green sock? ______

22. What is the probability of pulling out a yellow sock? ______

Indicate whether the probability outcome is "impossible," "unlikely," "equally likely," "likely," or "certain."

23. The outcome with a probability of $\frac{3}{4}$ is ________________________.

24. The outcome with a probability of $\frac{5}{5}$ is ________________________.

25. The outcome with a probability of $\frac{1}{8}$ is ________________________.

NAME ____________________

Lesson 11.1 Reading Picture Graphs

A **picture graph** uses symbols to represent data.

The key tells you the value of each symbol on the picture graph.

How many students have red hair color?

Students' Hair Color

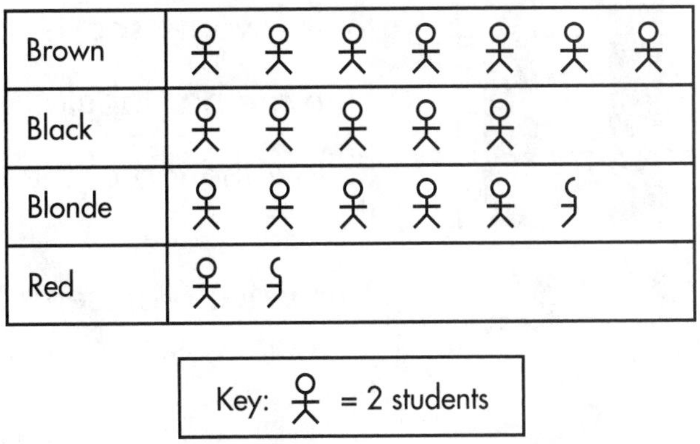

Brown	웃 웃 웃 웃 웃 웃 웃
Black	웃 웃 웃 웃 웃
Blonde	웃 웃 웃 웃 웃 ½웃
Red	웃 ½웃

Key: 웃 = 2 students

Each stick figure represents two students.

Count by twos when counting the stick figures in the row labeled "red." Add 1 to the sum for the half stick figure.

__3__ students have red hair.

Use the picture graph to answer each question.

1. What hair color do the most students have? ____________

2. What hair color do the fewest students have? ____________

3. How many students have black hair? ____________

4. How many students have blonde hair? ____________

5. What hair color do 14 students have? ____________

NAME ___________________________

Lesson 11.2 Reading Bar Graphs

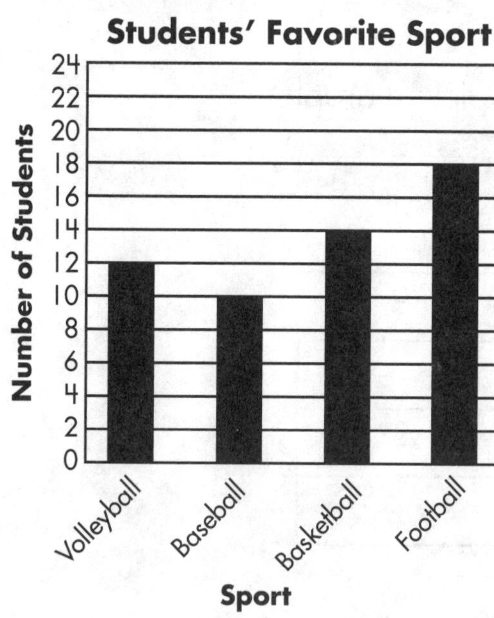

A **bar graph** uses rectangular bars to represent data.

The scale of a bar graph helps you identify the value of each bar.

How many students chose baseball as their favorite sport?

Find the bar labeled baseball.

Follow the top of the bar to the scale at the left.

This value represents the number of students whose favorite sport is baseball.

<u>10</u> students chose baseball as their favorite sport.

Use the bar graph to answer each question.

1. Which sport did most students choose as their favorite? __________

2. Which sport did the fewest students choose as their favorite? __________

3. Which sport did 14 students choose as their favorite? __________

4. How many students chose volleyball as their favorite sport? __________

5. How many students chose football as their favorite sport? __________

6. What is the difference between the most favorite and the least favorite sport? __________

7. How many sports are recorded? __________

NAME ____________________

Lesson 11.3 Line Graphs

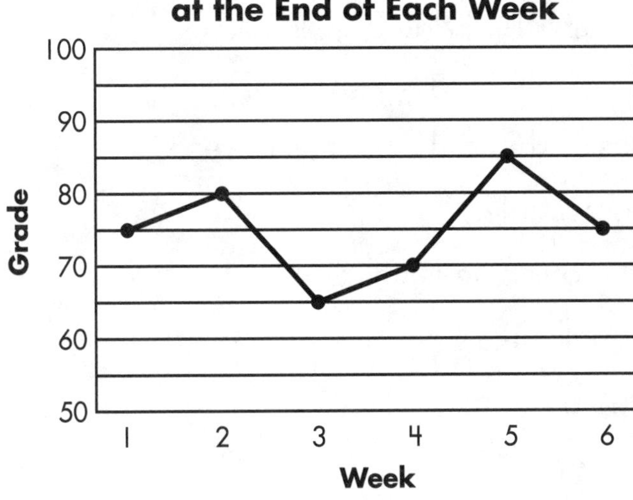

A **line graph** uses a line to show how data changes over a period of time.

Each point on the graph represents a data value at a given time.

What was Lucinda's grade in math class at the end of week 4?

Locate the point that represents the end of week 4. Follow this point to the scale at the left. This value represents Lucinda's grade at the end of week 4.

Lucinda had a grade of <u>70</u> at the end of week 4.

Use the line graph to answer each question.

1. Which week was Lucinda's math grade the highest? __________
2. Which week was Lucinda's math grade the lowest? __________
3. What was Lucinda's week 1 grade? __________
4. What was Lucinda's week 3 grade? __________
5. Were the grades for any weeks the same? If so, which weeks? __________
6. Which week did Lucinda have a math grade of 80? __________
7. Which week did Lucinda have a math grade of 85? __________

NAME ____________________

Lesson 11.4 Probability

Probability is the chance of an event occurring.

$$\text{Probability of an event} = \frac{\text{number of favorable outcomes}}{\text{total number of possible outcomes}}$$

What is the probability that Jane's birthday is in June?

$$\frac{\text{number of favorable outcomes}}{\text{total number of possible outcomes}} = \frac{1}{12} \begin{array}{l} \leftarrow 1 \text{ month in year} \\ \leftarrow 12 \text{ months in year} \end{array}$$

If the probability is 0, then the outcome is impossible.

If the probability is between 0 and $\frac{1}{2}$, then the outcome is unlikely.

If the probability is $\frac{1}{2}$, then the outcome is equally likely.

If the probability is between $\frac{1}{2}$ and 1, then the outcome is likely.

If the probability is 1, then the outcome is certain.

What is the probability of

rolling a 7 on a 6-sided die?	rolling a 1 on a 6-sided die?	rolling a 1, 2, 3, or 4 on a 6-sided die?	rolling a 1, 2, 3, 4, 5, or 6 on a 6-sided die?
$\frac{0}{6} = 0$	$\frac{1}{6}$	$\frac{4}{6}$	$\frac{6}{6} = 1$
"impossible"	"unlikely"	"likely"	"certain"

Write the correct probability for the following. Indicate whether the outcome is "impossible," "unlikely," "equally likely," "likely," or "certain."

1. What is the probability of flipping a coin and getting a heads or tails? $\frac{2}{2}$ certain
2. What is the probability of flipping a coin and getting heads? ____ ________
3. What is the probability that Lenny's birthday is in a month starting with the letter M? (A calendar appears on p. 132.) ____ ________
4. What is the probability that Arnold's birthday is in a month that does *not* start with the letter J? ____ ________
5. What is the probability of rolling a 1, 3, 4, 5, or 6 on a six-sided die? ____ ________

NAME ____________________

Check What You Learned

Graphs and Probability

Use the picture graph to answer each question.

Students' Birthday Month

January	🎁 🎁 🎁
February	🎁
March	🎁 ½🎁
April	🎁 🎁 🎁 🎁
May	
June	
July	🎁
August	🎁
September	🎁 ½🎁
October	
November	🎁 🎁 ½🎁
December	🎁 🎁 🎁 ½🎁

Key: 🎁 = 2 students

1. In which month(s) are there no student birthdays? ____________________

2. How many students have a birthday in January? ________

3. How many students have a birthday in July? ________

4. In which month do most students have their birthday? ____________

5. How many more students have their birthday in December than in September? ____________

6. Five students have their birthday in which month? ____________

7. Three students have their birthday in which month(s)? ____________

Use the bar graph to answer each question.

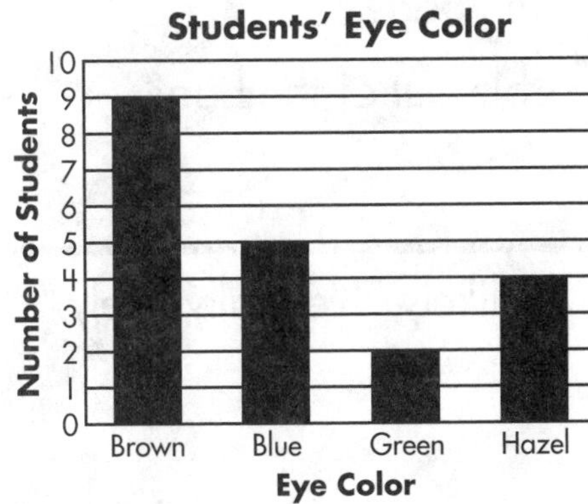

8. How many students have blue eyes? ________

9. What eye color do most students have? ________

10. What eye color do the fewest students have? ________

11. Four students have what eye color? ________

12. Nine students have what eye color? ________

13. How many students have green eyes? ________

NAME ______________________

Check What You Learned

Graphs and Probability

Use the line graph to answer each question.

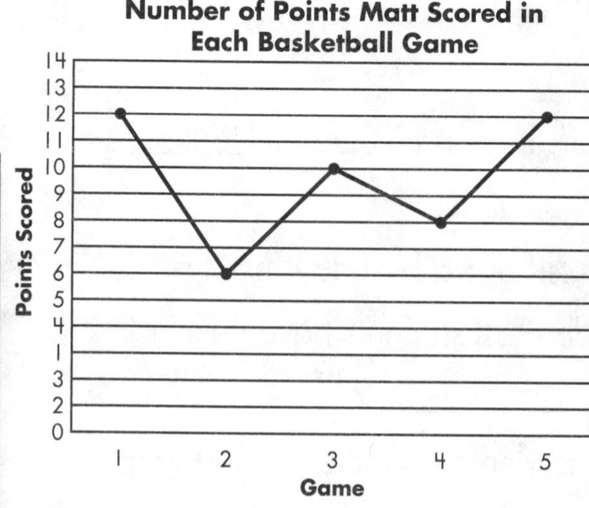

14. In which game(s) did Matt score the most points? ________

15. In which game did Matt score the fewest points? ________

16. How many total points did Matt score for all five games? ________

17. In which game did Matt score 6 points? ________

18. In which game did Matt score 10 points? ________

19. How many points did Matt score in game 1? ________

Write the correct probability for the following.

In a bag, there are 3 red marbles, 6 blue marbles, 2 white marbles, and 1 black marble.

20. What is the probability of pulling a blue marble out of the bag? ________

21. What is the probability of pulling a red marble out of the bag? ________

22. What is the probability of pulling a white or black marble out of the bag?

____

Indicate whether the probability outcome is "impossible," "unlikely," "equally likely," "likely," or "certain."

23. The outcome with a probability of $\frac{6}{6}$ is ________.

24. The outcome with a probability of $\frac{0}{3}$ is ________.

25. The outcome with a probability of $\frac{5}{6}$ is ________.

Check What You Know

Geometry

Match each figure in column a with its name in column b.

	a	b
1. ______		A. circle
2. ______		B. cube
3. ______	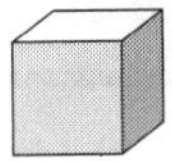	C. rectangle
4. ______		D. sphere
5. ______	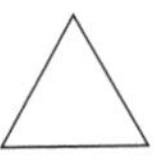	E. square
6. ______	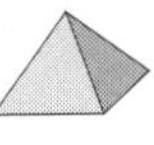	F. square pyramid
7. ______		G. triangle

Label each figure as solid or plane.

	a	b	c	d	e
8.	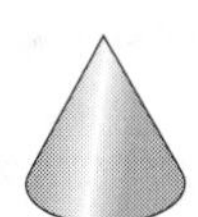		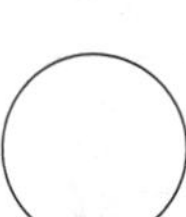	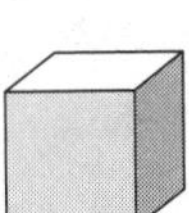	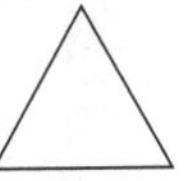
	______	______	______	______	______

Complete each table.

	Figure	Number of Sides	Number of Square Corners	Number of Other Corners
9.	square			
10.	circle			
11.	rectangle			

	Figure	Number of Square Faces	Number of Triangle Faces	Number of Rectangle Faces	Number of Edges
12.	cube				
13.	square pyramid				
14.	sphere				

NAME ____________________

Check What You Know

Geometry

Indicate if the figures are congruent or not congruent.

15.

a	b	c	d
 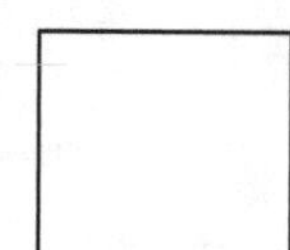	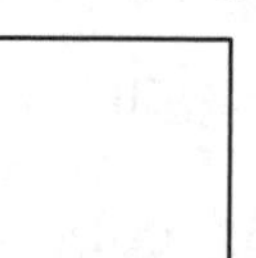	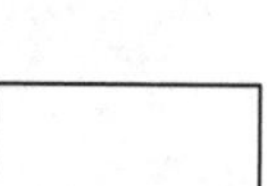	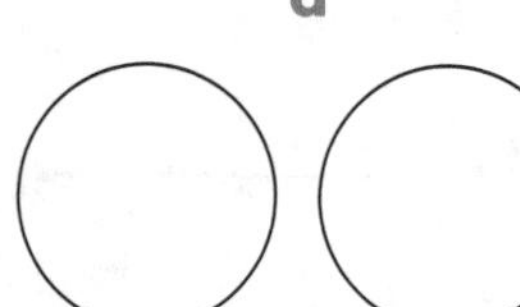
________	________	________	________

Indicate if the objects are not symmetrical or symmetrical.
If the object is symmetrical, draw the line of symmetry.

16.

a	b	c	d
		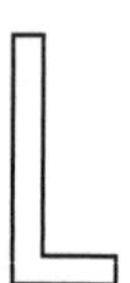	
________	________	________	________

Is the line drawn on each figure a line of symmetry?

17.

a	b	c	d
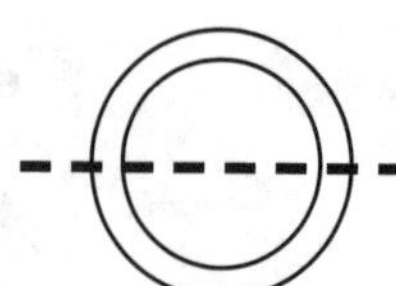	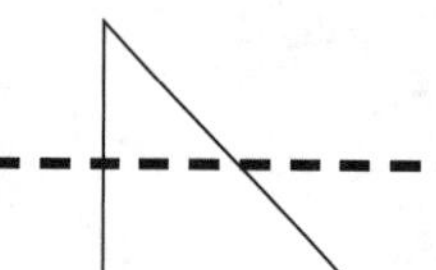		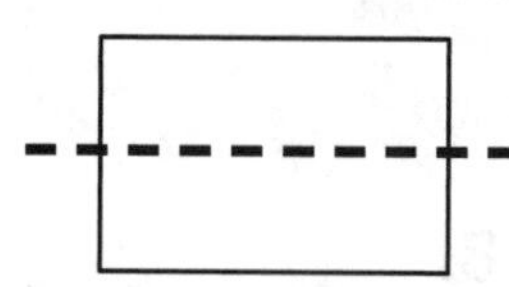
________	________	________	________

Identify each figure as a point, line, line segment, ray, or angle.
Name each figure.

18.

a	b	c	d
	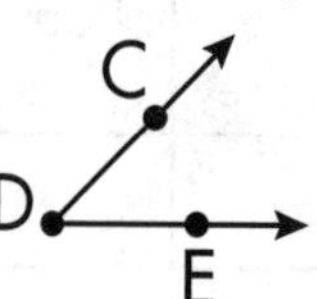	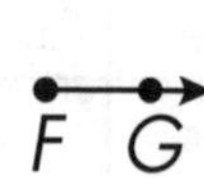	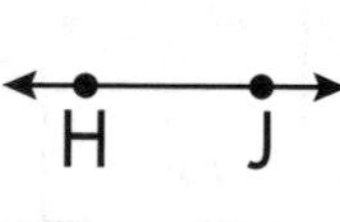
________	________	________	________
________	________	________	________

NAME ____________________

Lesson 12.1 Plane Figures

A **plane figure** is a flat surface.

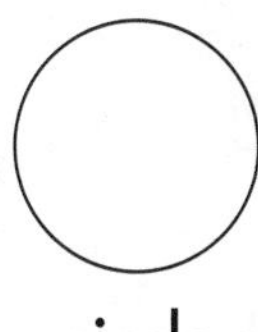
circle

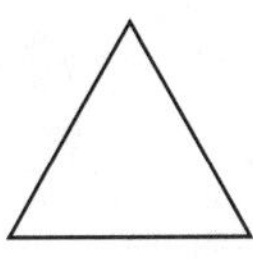
triangle

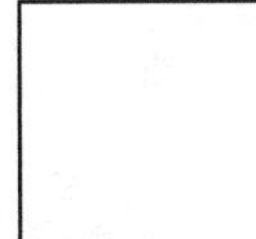
square

rectangle

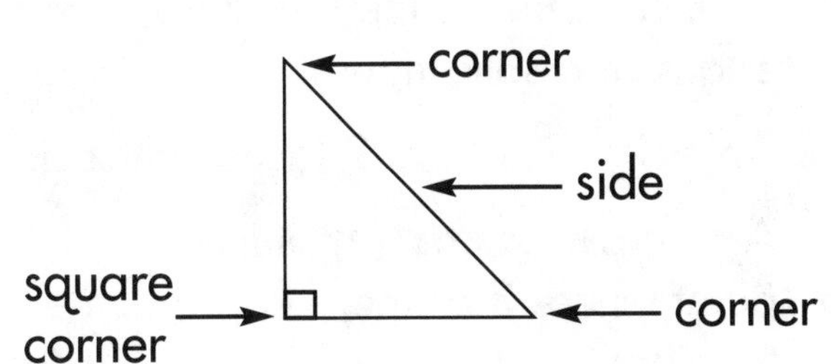

Each side of a triangle, square, and rectangle is a **line segment**.

The point where two line segments meet is a **corner** or a **square corner**.

A square corner is a right angle. A right angle has a measure of 90°.

Draw the following plane figures.

	a	b	c	d
1.	triangle	rectangle	square	circle

Complete the following.

	a	b	c	d	e
	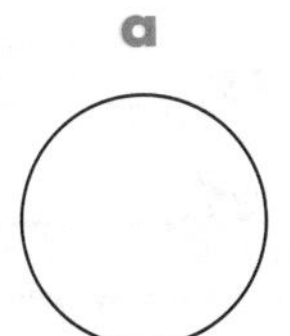	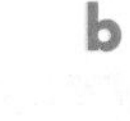	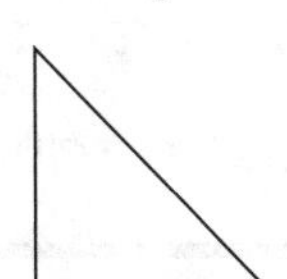	 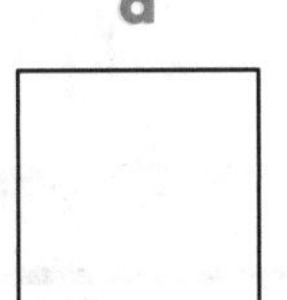	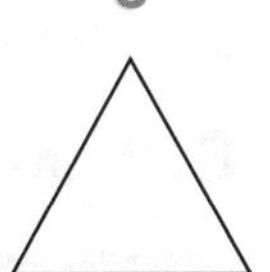
2. number of sides	0	______	______	______	______
3. number of square corners	______	______	1	______	0
4. number of other corners	______	______	______	______	______

Lesson 12.2 Solid Figures

A **solid figure** is a three-dimensional object. Solid figures may be hollow or solid.

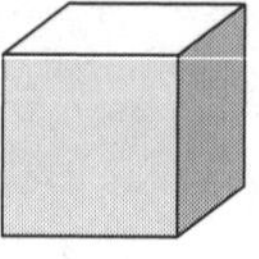

cube

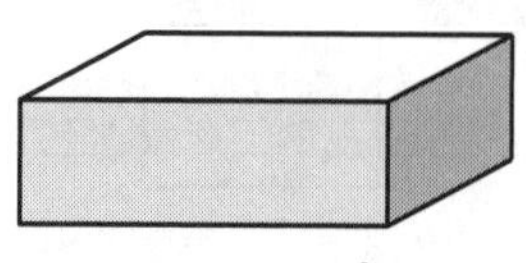

rectangular prism

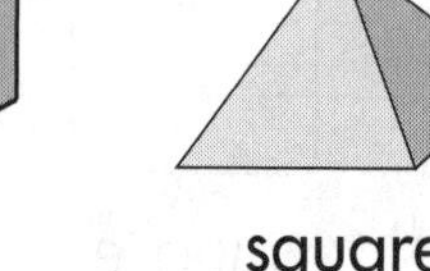

square pyramid

sphere

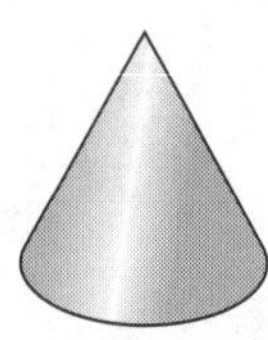

cylinder

cone

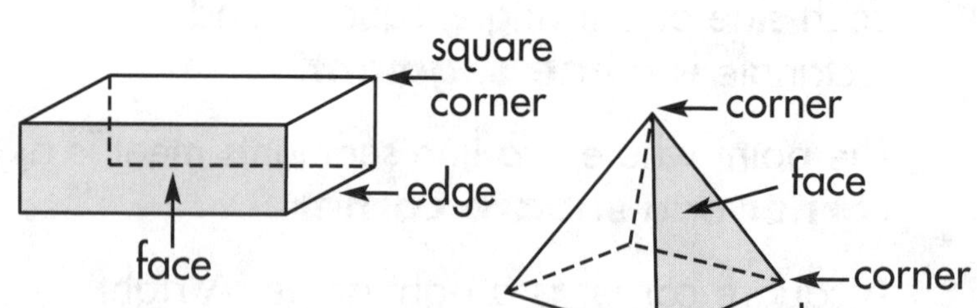

A **face** is the shape formed by the edges of a solid figure.

An **edge** is where 2 faces intersect.

A **vertex** or **corner** is the point where 3 or more edges come together.

Complete the table.

	Solid Figure	Number of Square Faces	Number of Rectangle Faces	Number of Triangle Faces
1.	cube			0
2.	rectangular prism			
3.	square pyramid	1		

4. How many edges does a sphere have? _____ edges

5. How many edges does a square pyramid have? _____ edges

6. How many edges does a cube have? _____ edges

7. How many edges does a rectangular prism have? _____ edges

8. How many corners does a square pyramid have? _____ corners

Give a physical example of each of the following plane figures.

	a	b	c
9.	cube sugar cube	rectangular prism ______	square pyramid ______
10.	sphere ______	cylinder ______	cone ______

NAME ____________________

Lesson 12.3 Comparing Figures

Label each the figure as plane or solid.

	a	b	c	d
1.	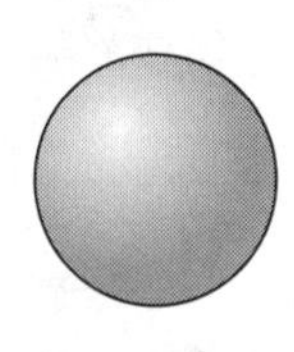	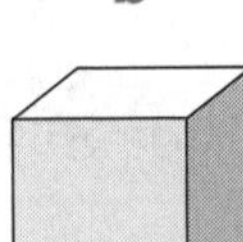		
	solid	______	______	______
2.	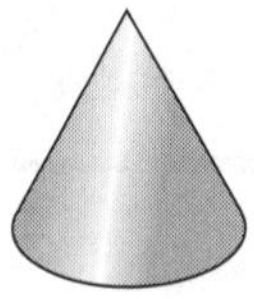		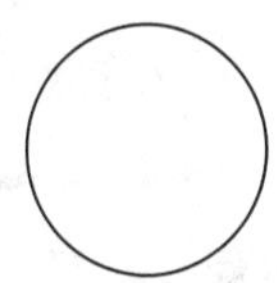	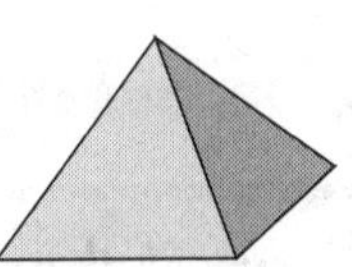
	______	______	______	______

Match the solid figures with the plane figures that are shaped most like them. Answers may be used more than once.

B **3.** 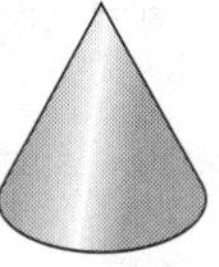

______ **4.** 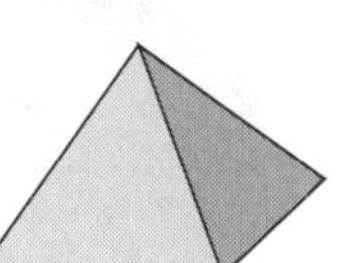

______ **5.** 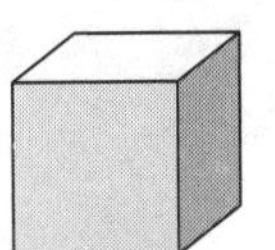

______ **6.** 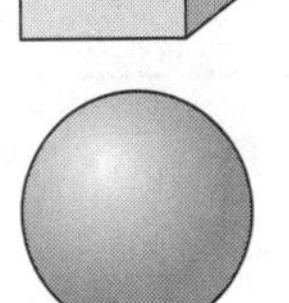

______ **7.**

______ **8.**

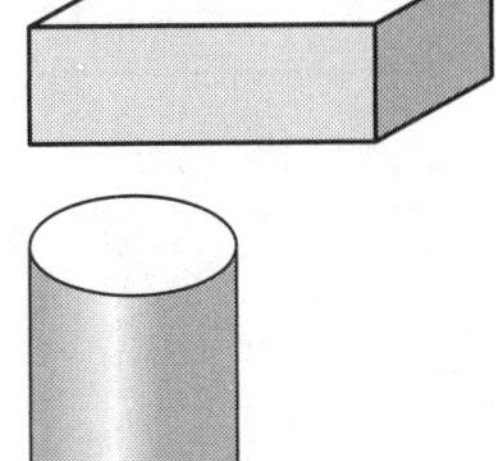

A. 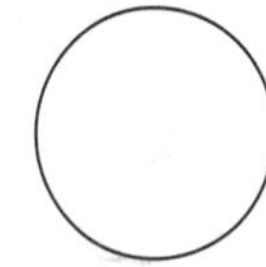

B. 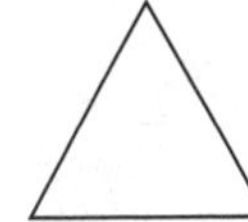

C. 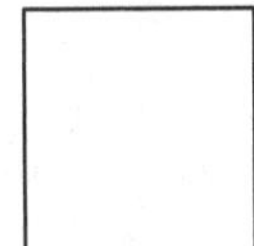

D. 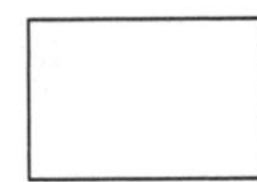

NAME ______________________

Lesson 12.4 Congruent Shapes

Congruent figures have exactly the same shape and size.

Is a □ congruent to a △ ? Why or why not?

No, because a square and a triangle are different shapes.

Is ◺ congruent to △ ? Why or why not?

No, because the two triangles are not exactly the same shape.

Is □ congruent to □ ? Why or why not?

Yes, because they are exactly the same shape and size.

Indicate if these figures are congruent or not congruent.

a b c d

1. 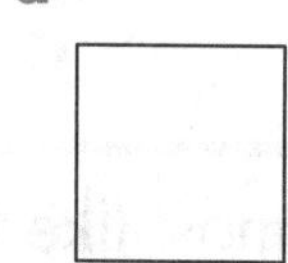 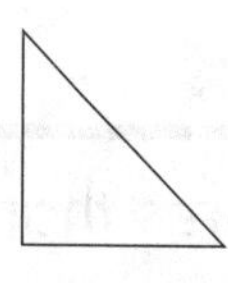 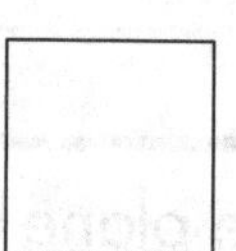 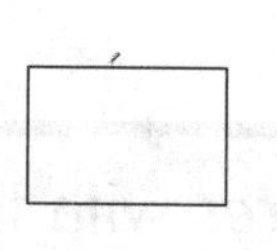  

not congruent ______ ______ ______

2.  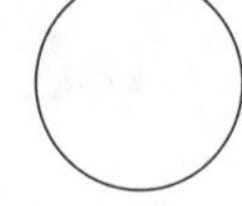   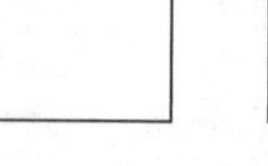 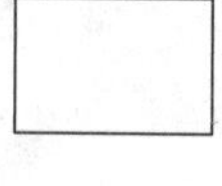 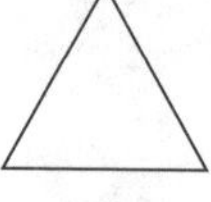 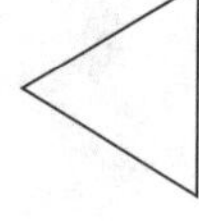 

______ ______ ______ ______

3.  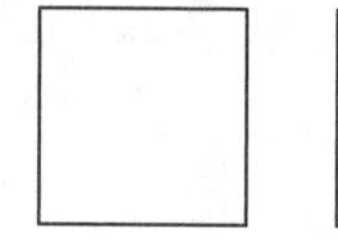 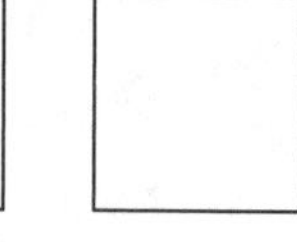   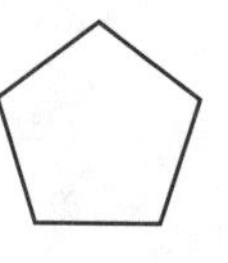 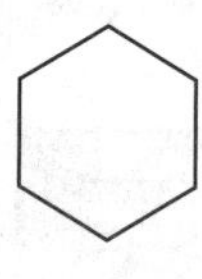 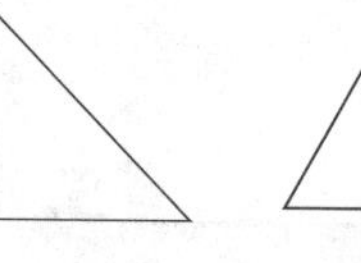

______ ______ ______ ______

4. 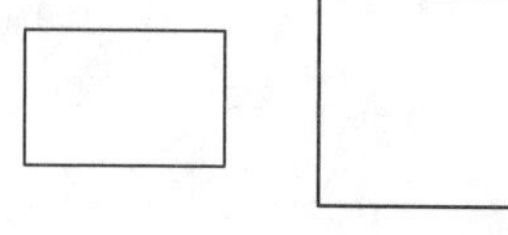 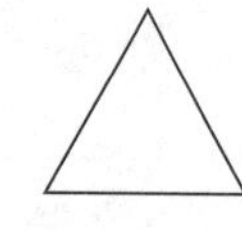 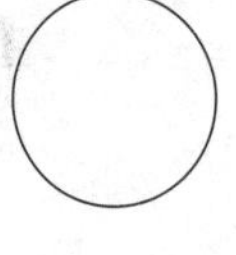  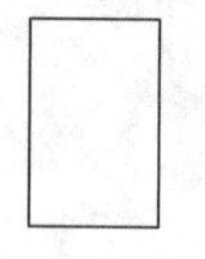 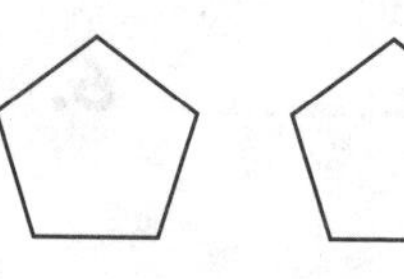

______ ______ ______ ______

5.  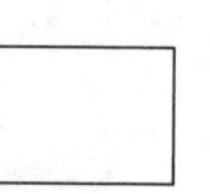 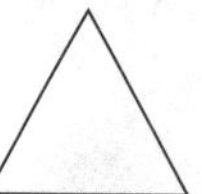   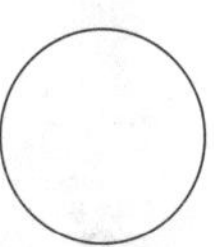 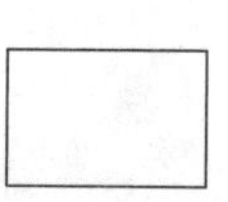

______ ______ ______ ______

NAME ______________________

Lesson 12.5 Symmetrical Shapes

A figure or a shape is **symmetrical** when one-half of the figure is the mirror image of the other half.

A **line of symmetry** divides a figure or shape into two halves that are congruent.

The letter A is symmetrical.

The letter A has one line of symmetry.

The letter O is symmetrical.

The letter O has many lines of symmetry.

The letter F is not symmetrical.

The letter F does not have a line of symmetry.

Is the line drawn on each figure a line of symmetry?

	a	b	c	d
1.	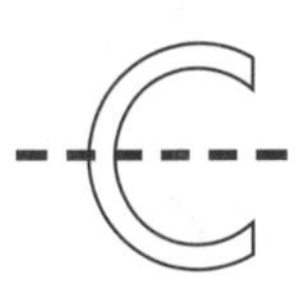 ______	______	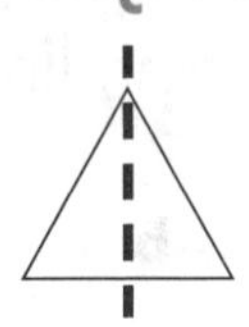 ______	no
2.	 ______	 ______	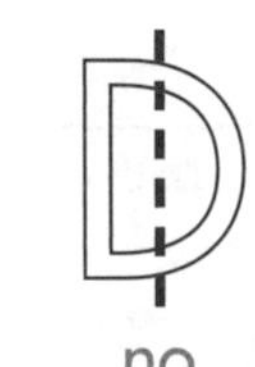 no	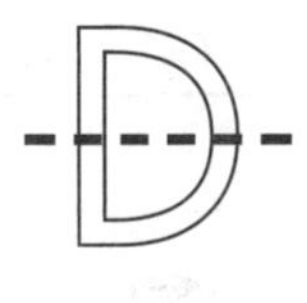 ______

Label each figure as not symmetrical or symmetrical. If the figure is symmetrical, draw the line (or lines) of symmetry.

	a	b	c	d
3.	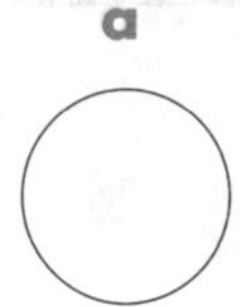 ______	 ______	 ______	 ______
4.	 ______	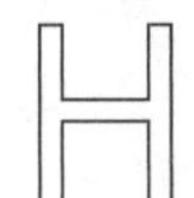 ______	 ______	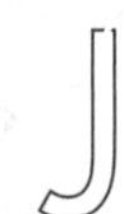 ______

NAME ______________________

Lesson 12.6 Line Segments

	Figure	Definition	Dimension	How to Name Each Figure
point	• *A*	An exact location in space.	no length no width	A, capital letter
line	*C* *D*	A collection of points going on and on in both directions. Arrowheads indicate infinite length.	length no width	$\overleftrightarrow{CD}$
line segment	*X* *Y*	A part of a line. Two endpoints and the collection of points between the endpoints.	length no width	$\overline{XY}$
ray		A part of a line. One endpoint and the rest of the line that goes on and on.	length no width	$\overrightarrow{FG}$

J *K* 2 *L*

An **angle** is formed by two rays with a common endpoint. This endpoint is called a **vertex**. This angle is named ∠*JKL*, ∠*K*, or ∠2. Angles are found wherever lines and line segments intersect.

Identify each figure as a point, line, line segment, ray, or angle.
Name each figure.

	a	b	c	d	e
1.	*A* *B*	• *P*	• *Q*	3	*X* *Y*
	line segment	point	______	______	______
	$\overline{AB}$	P	______	______	______
2.	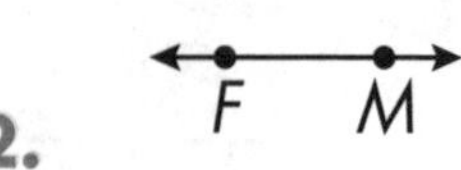	*R* *S*	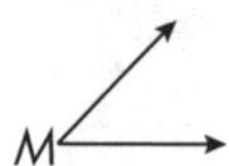	*T* *V* *W*	
	______	______	______	______	______
	______	______	______	______	______

Identify the parts of this angle.

3. The vertex is point __________.

4. $\overrightarrow{XY}$ is a __________.

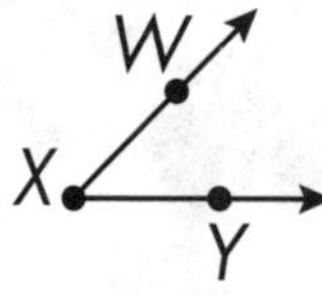

Use a ruler, if necessary, to draw these items.

	a	b	c	d	e
5.	line	line segment	ray	angle	point
	______	______	______	______	______

NAME ____________________

Check What You Learned

Geometry

CHAPTER 12 POSTTEST

Name each figure. Label each figure as solid or plane.

	a	b	c	d
1.			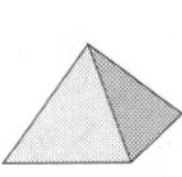	
2.	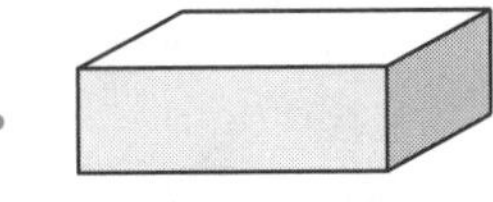		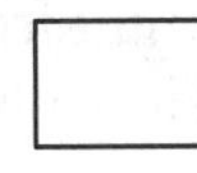	
3.	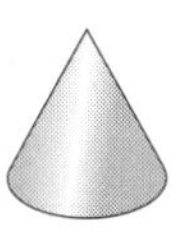	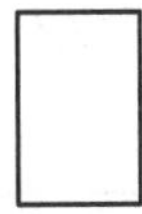	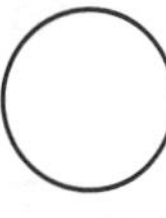	

How many sides or edges are there on these figures?

	a	b	c	d
4.		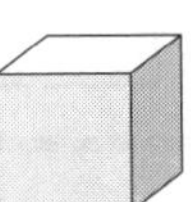	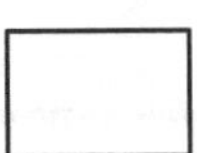	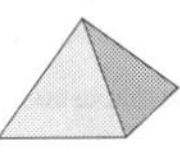

How many faces are on each figure?

	a	b	c	d
5.	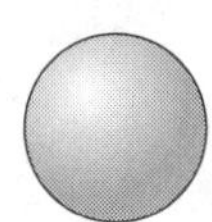	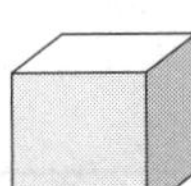		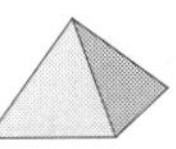

NAME ____________________

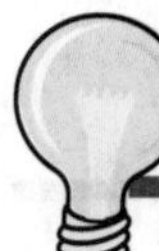

Check What You Learned

Geometry

Indicate if the figures are congruent or not congruent.

	a	b	c	d
6.	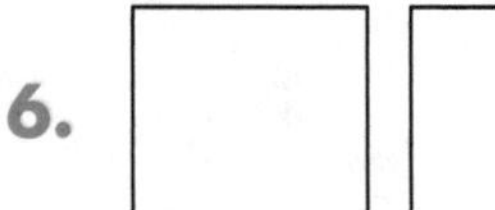		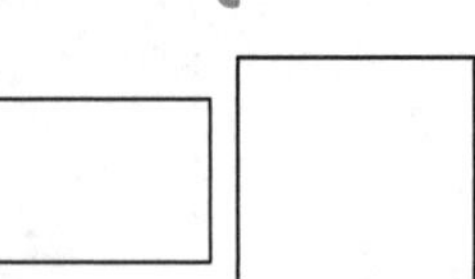	
	________	________	________	________

Indicate if the objects are symmetrical or not symmetrical.
If the object is symmetrical, draw the line of symmetry.

	a	b	c	d
7.		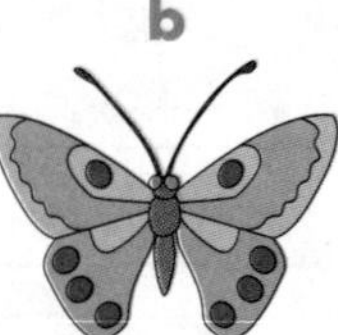		
	________	________	________	________

Is the line drawn on each figure a line of symmetry?

	a	b	c	d
8.	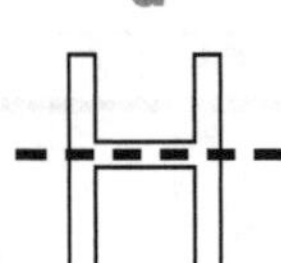	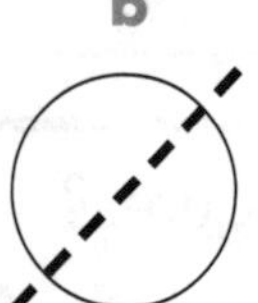	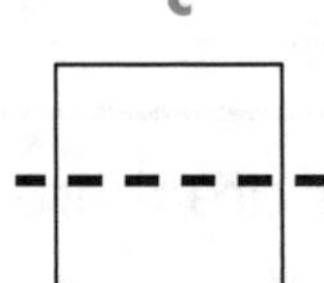	
	________	________	________	________

Match each figure with its description.

9.	____	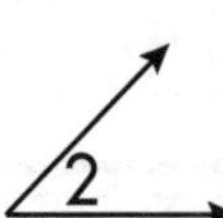	A. point
10.	____	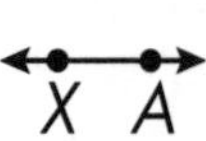	B. angle
11.	____		C. ray
12.	____	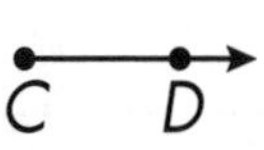	D. line

Match each figure with its name.

13.	____		G. ∠GHJ
14.	____		H. $\overline{AB}$
15.	____	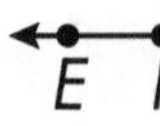	I. $\overrightarrow{CD}$
16.	____	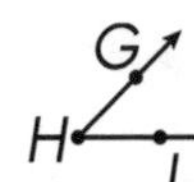	J. $\overleftrightarrow{EF}$

NAME ______________________

Check What You Know

Preparing for Algebra

Complete the pattern.

1.

____

____

____

Write the number of objects under each group of objects.

	a	b	c	d	e
2.	○ ○	○ ○ ○ ○		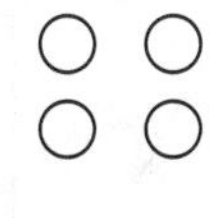	○ ○
	______	______	______	______	______
3.	△ △ △ △ △	△ △ △ △	△ △ △	△ △	△
	______	______	______	______	______
4.	□		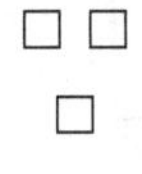	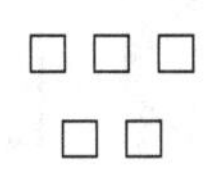	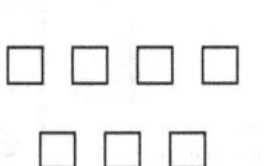
	______	______	______	______	______

Complete the pattern by using addition or subtraction.

				a	b	c	d
5.	30	26	22	____	____	____	____
6.	1	2	3	____	____	____	____
7.	5	10	15	____	____	____	____
8.	4	8	16	____	____	____	____
9.	1	3	5	____	____	____	____
10.	10	9	8	____	____	____	____

NAME ________________

CHAPTER 13 PRETEST

Check What You Know

Preparing for Algebra

Complete each repeating geometric pattern.

				a	b	c
11.	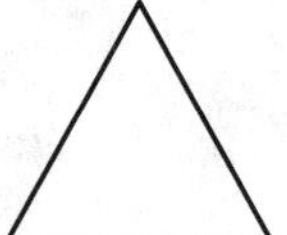		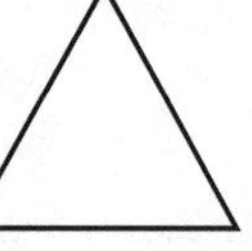	________	________	________
12.	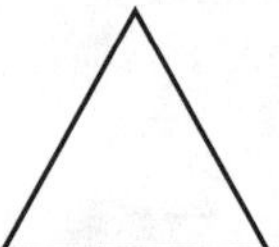	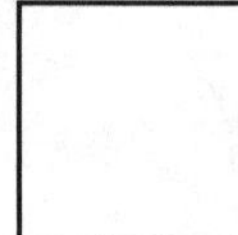	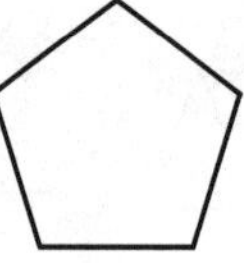	________	________	________
13.	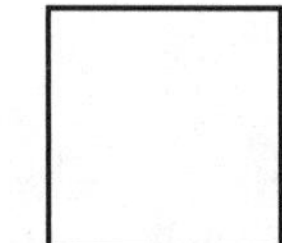	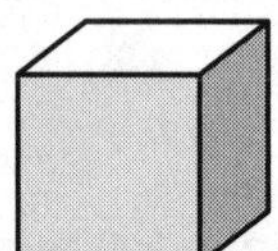		________	________	________

Complete the following.

	a	b	c	d
14.	$3 + \square = 3$	$5 + 0 = \square$	$7 \times 1 = \square$	$\square \times 1 = 6$
15.	$5 + 4 = 9$ or $5 + 4 = 2 + \square$	$6 + 9 = 15$ or $6 + 9 = 10 + \square$	$2 \times 9 = 18$ or $2 \times 9 = 6 \times \square$	$4 \times 5 = 20$ or $4 \times 5 = 10 \times \square$

Write the number sentence. For the missing part, use a box ($\square$). Solve each number sentence.

16. The sum of two and three is what number? ________

The sum of the two and three is ________.

17. The product of five and four is what number? ________

The product of five and four is ________.

18. Ten minus eight is what number? ________

Ten minus eight is ________.

NAME ____________________

Lesson 13.1 Patterns

Start at the top of each column and work down. Complete each pattern.

1.     ____________ ____________ ____________

2. 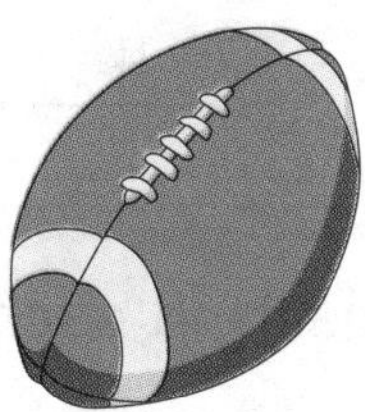 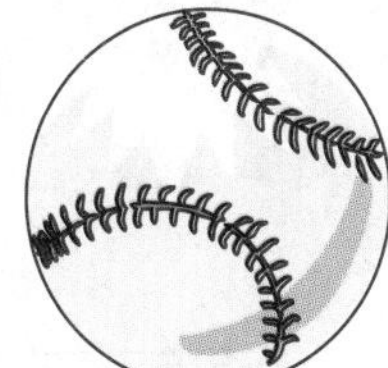  ____________ ____________ ____________

3.   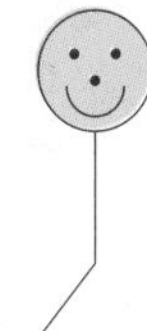 ____________ ____________ ____________

4.  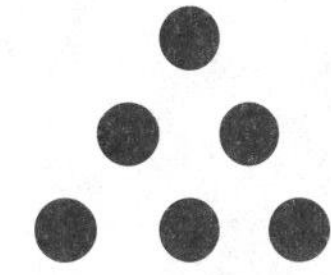 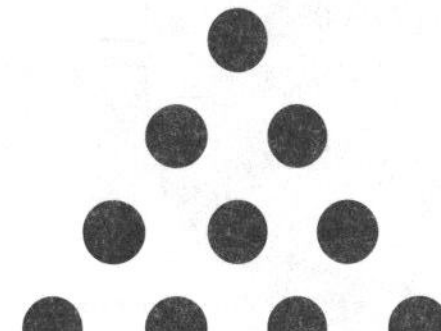 ____________ ____________ ____________

5.    ____________ ____________ ____________

NAME ____________________

Lesson 13.2 Transferring Patterns

•　　••　　•••　　••••　　•••••

1　　2　　3　　4　　5

Write the number of objects under each group of objects in each pattern.

	a	b	c	d	e
1.					
	______	______	______	______	______
2.	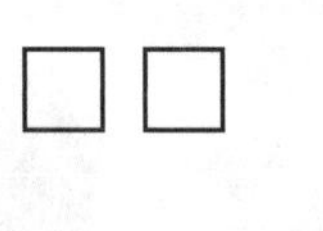	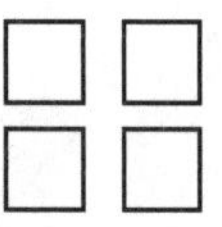		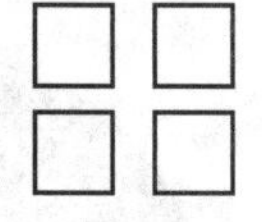	
	______	______	______	______	______
3.			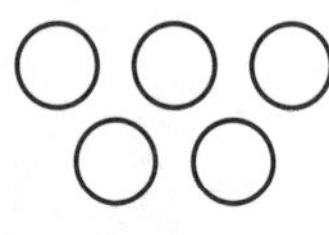	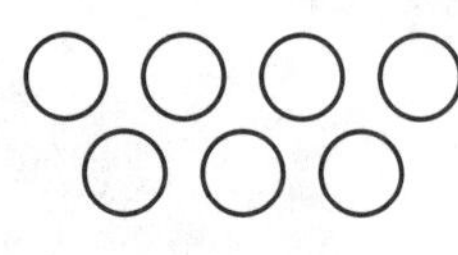	
	______	______	______	______	______
4.			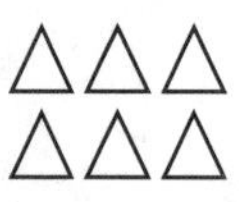	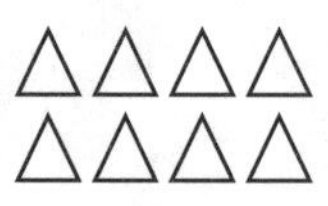	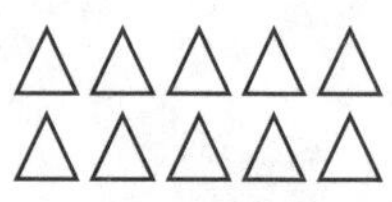
	______	______	______	______	______
5.		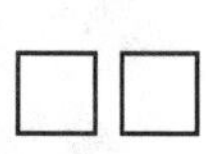		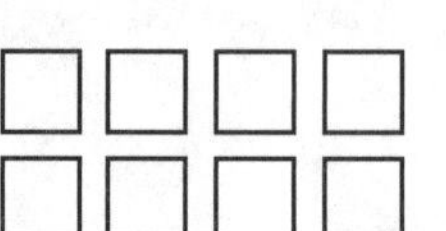	
	______	______	______	______	______

NAME ______________________

Lesson 13.3 Number Patterns

A number pattern can be developed by addition or subtraction.

Complete this pattern by subtraction.

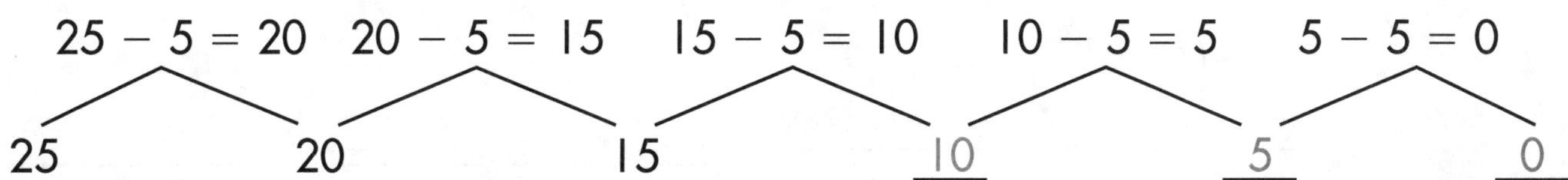

Complete the pattern by using addition or subtraction.

				a	b	c
1.	2	4	6	8	10	12
2.	1	3	5	____	____	____
3.	20	18	16	____	____	____
4.	21	15	10	____	____	____
5.	13	12	11	____	____	____
6.	5	10	15	____	____	____
7.	3	6	9	____	____	____
8.	10	20	40	____	____	____
9.	16	13	10	____	____	____
10.	10	9	8	____	____	____

NAME ______________________

Lesson 13.4 Geometric Patterns

Complete each repeating geometric pattern.

				a	b	c
1.	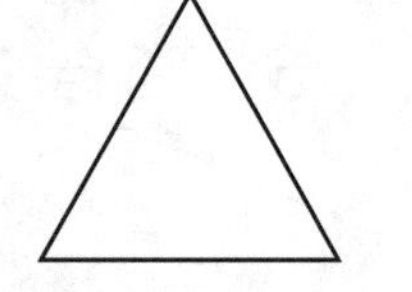		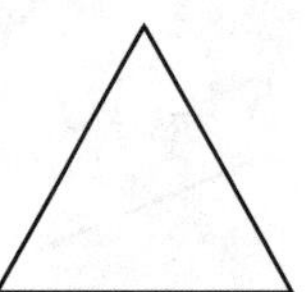	______	______	______
2.			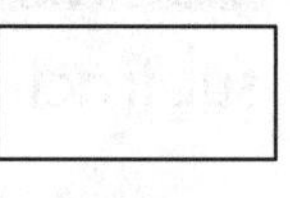	______	______	______
3.	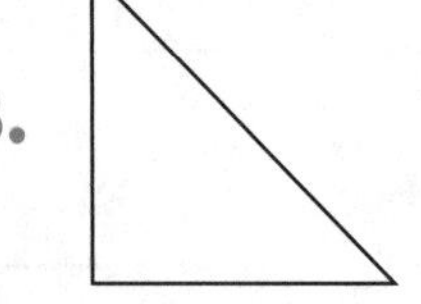		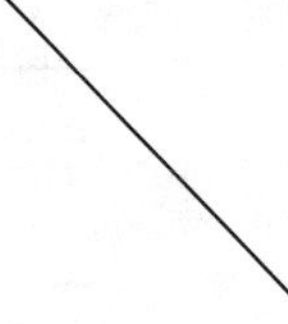	______	______	______
4.	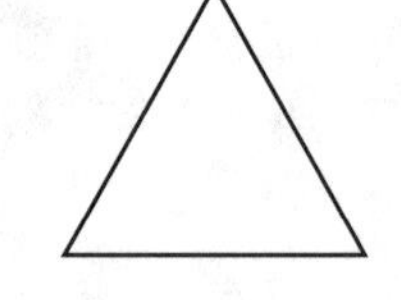	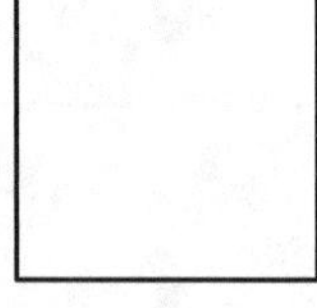	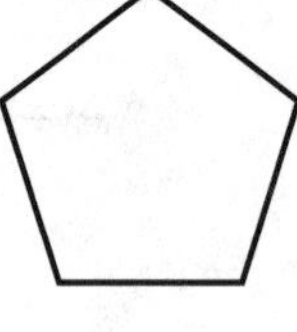	______	______	______
5.	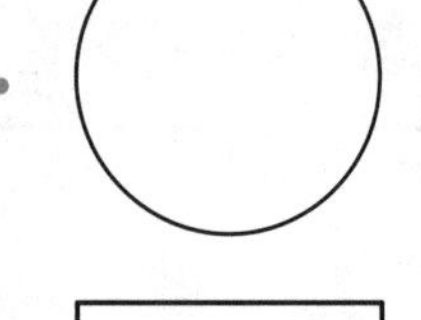		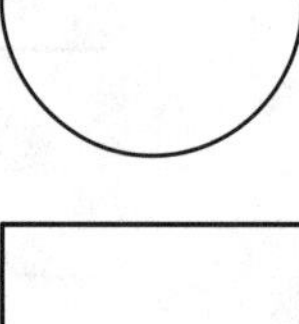	______	______	______
6.				______	______	______
7.	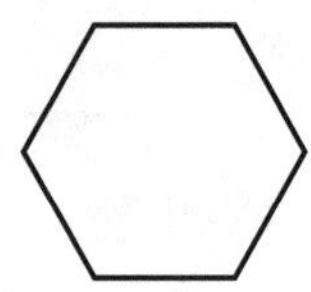	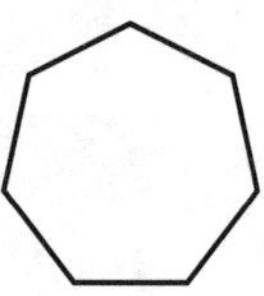	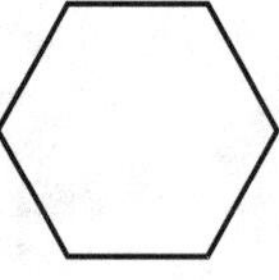	______	______	______
8.		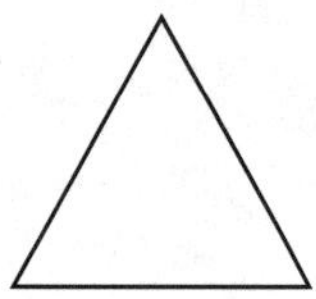		______	______	______

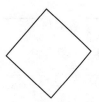

NAME ______________________

Lesson 13.5 Number Sentences

A **number sentence** is an equation with numbers.

Identity Property		**Commutative Property**	
for addition:	$0 + 3 = 3$	for addition:	$3 + 2 = 2 + 3$
for multiplication:	$1 \times 3 = 3$	for multiplication:	$4 \times 2 = 2 \times 4$

A number sentence can change its look but not change its value.

$3 + 5 = 8$ or $3 + 5 = 4 + 4$ $3 \times 8 = 24$ or $3 \times 8 = 6 \times 4$

Complete each number sentence.

	a	b	c	d
1.	$0 + 4 = \boxed{4}$	$0 + 6 = \square$	$\square + 2 = 2$	$\square + 7 = 7$
2.	$1 \times 2 = \square$	$1 \times 5 = \square$	$\square \times 4 = 4$	$\square \times 9 = 9$
3.	$7 + 2 = \square + 7$	$3 + 4 = \square + 3$	$1 + 2 = 2 + \square$	$\square + 5 = 5 + 4$
4.	$5 \times 7 = 7 \times \square$	$4 \times \square = 3 \times 4$	$\square \times 3 = 3 \times 5$	$9 \times 4 = \square \times 9$

Complete the following.

	a	b	c	d
5.	$2 + 7 = 9$ or $2 + 7 = 5 + \boxed{4}$	$5 + 7 = 12$ or $5 + 7 = 6 + \square$	$4 + 3 = 7$ or $4 + 3 = 5 + \square$	$6 + 9 = 15$ or $6 + 9 = 10 + \square$
6.	$6 + 4 = 10$ or $6 + 4 = 5 + \square$	$6 + 7 = 13$ or $6 + 7 = 8 + \square$	$5 + 3 = 8$ or $5 + 3 = 6 + \square$	$9 + 2 = 11$ or $9 + 2 = 5 + \square$
7.	$5 \times 6 = 30$ or $5 \times 6 = 10 \times \boxed{3}$	$4 \times 3 = 12$ or $4 \times 3 = 2 \times \square$	$6 \times 3 = 18$ or $6 \times 3 = 9 \times \square$	$6 \times 2 = 12$ or $6 \times 2 = 4 \times \square$

NAME ____________________

Lesson 13.5 Problem Solving

Math Symbol	Key Words
$=$	is, is equal to, equals
$+$	added to, sum, and, plus
$-$	subtracted from, difference, minus
$\times$	multiplied by, the product of, times
$\div$	divided by

Write each number sentence. Put a box (□) in the sentence for the missing part. Solve each number sentence.

1. The sum of two and three is what number? $2 + 3 = \boxed{5}$
   The sum of the two and three is five.

2. Seven minus two is what number? __________
   Seven minus two is __________.

3. Four times three is what number? __________
   Four times three is __________.

4. Fourteen divided by two is what number? __________
   Fourteen divided by two is __________.

5. Five added to what number is seven? __________
   Five added to __________ is seven.

6. Thirteen minus what number is ten? __________
   Thirteen minus __________ is ten.

NAME ______________________

Check What You Learned

Preparing for Algebra

Complete the pattern.

1\. 

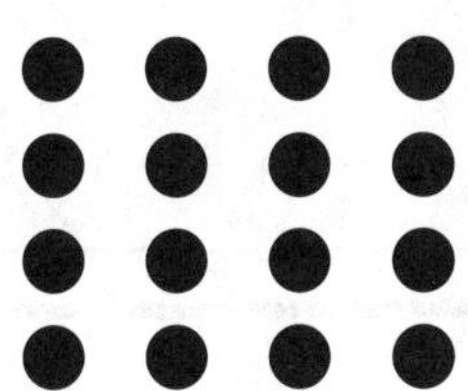

______

______

______

Write the number of objects under each group.

	a	b	c	d	e
2.	○	○ ○	○ ○ ○	○ ○ ○ ○	○ ○ ○ ○ ○
	______	______	______	______	______
3.	△△△△△ △△△△△	△△△△ △△△△	△△△ △△△	△△ △△	△ △
	______	______	______	______	______
4.	□□□□□ □□□□□	□□□□□ □□□□	□□□□ □□□	□□ □□	
	______	______	______	______	______

Complete the pattern by using addition or subtraction.

				a	b	c	d
5.	1	2	3	____	____	____	____
6.	50	45	40	____	____	____	____
7.	100	90	80	____	____	____	____
8.	4	8	12	____	____	____	____
9.	2	4	6	____	____	____	____
10.	33	35	37	____	____	____	____

CHAPTER 13 POSTTEST

Check What You Learned

Preparing for Algebra

Complete each repeating geometric pattern.

				a	b	c
11.	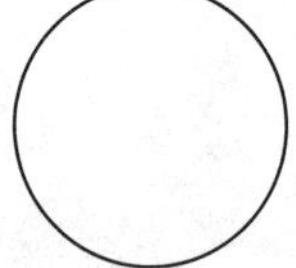		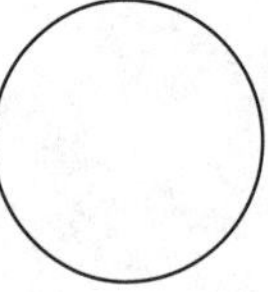	________	________	________
12.	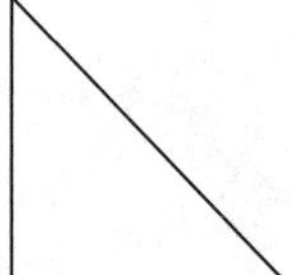		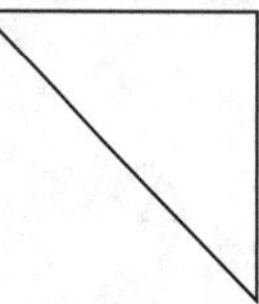	________	________	________
13.	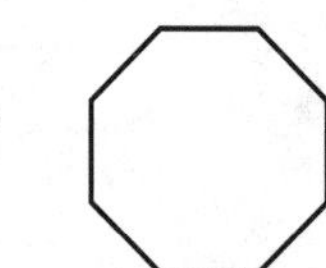	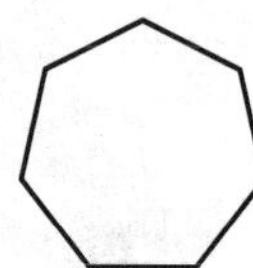	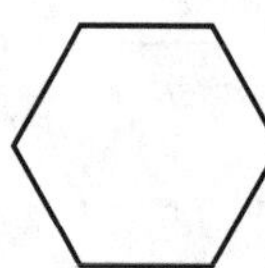	________	________	________

Complete the following.

	a	b	c	d
14.	5 + □ = 5	□ + 0 = 4	2 × 1 = □	3 × 1 = □
15.	2 + 7 = 9 or 2 + 7 = 6 + □	5 + 9 = 14 or 5 + 9 = 8 + □	3 × 8 = 24 or 3 × 8 = 4 × □	6 × 2 = 12 or 6 × 2 = 4 × □

Write each number sentence. For the missing part, use a box (□). Solve each number sentence.

16. Twelve divided by six is what number? __________

Twelve divided by six is __________.

17. Seven times three is what number? __________

Seven times three is __________.

18. Five plus six is what number? __________

Five plus six is __________.

NAME ____________________

Final Test Chapters 1–13

Add or subtract.

	a	b	c	d	e
1.	$\begin{array}{r} 9 \\ +4 \\ \hline \end{array}$	$\begin{array}{r} 3 \\ +19 \\ \hline \end{array}$	$\begin{array}{r} 21 \\ +42 \\ \hline \end{array}$	$\begin{array}{r} 67 \\ +29 \\ \hline \end{array}$	$\begin{array}{r} 57 \\ +\ \ 4 \\ \hline \end{array}$
2.	$\begin{array}{r} 319 \\ 23 \\ +152 \\ \hline \end{array}$	$\begin{array}{r} 59 \\ 63 \\ +142 \\ \hline \end{array}$	$\begin{array}{r} 57 \\ 59 \\ +63 \\ \hline \end{array}$	$\begin{array}{r} 403 \\ +907 \\ \hline \end{array}$	$\begin{array}{r} 500 \\ +320 \\ \hline \end{array}$
3.	$\begin{array}{r} 23 \\ -11 \\ \hline \end{array}$	$\begin{array}{r} 54 \\ -19 \\ \hline \end{array}$	$\begin{array}{r} 316 \\ -\ \ 23 \\ \hline \end{array}$	$\begin{array}{r} 594 \\ -\ \ 95 \\ \hline \end{array}$	$\begin{array}{r} 419 \\ -\ \ 21 \\ \hline \end{array}$
4.	$\begin{array}{r} 113 \\ -\ \ 92 \\ \hline \end{array}$	$\begin{array}{r} 54 \\ -13 \\ \hline \end{array}$	$\begin{array}{r} 8 \\ -7 \\ \hline \end{array}$	$\begin{array}{r} 46 \\ -32 \\ \hline \end{array}$	$\begin{array}{r} 511 \\ -\ \ 21 \\ \hline \end{array}$
5.	$\begin{array}{r} 1321 \\ +4923 \\ \hline \end{array}$	$\begin{array}{r} 6876 \\ +\ \ 192 \\ \hline \end{array}$	$\begin{array}{r} 541 \\ +962 \\ \hline \end{array}$	$\begin{array}{r} 5921 \\ +2543 \\ \hline \end{array}$	$\begin{array}{r} 3864 \\ +\ \ 193 \\ \hline \end{array}$
6.	$\begin{array}{r} 4321 \\ -\ \ 491 \\ \hline \end{array}$	$\begin{array}{r} 5963 \\ -1892 \\ \hline \end{array}$	$\begin{array}{r} 9876 \\ -7293 \\ \hline \end{array}$	$\begin{array}{r} 5434 \\ -\ \ 502 \\ \hline \end{array}$	$\begin{array}{r} 4732 \\ -1693 \\ \hline \end{array}$

SHOW YOUR WORK

Solve each problem.

7. In 1984, Mr. Alvin was 103 years old. What year was he born?

   Mr. Alvin was born in ____________.

8. Sandy spent 14 dollars of her 38 dollars on a radio. How much money does she have left?

   Sandy has ____________ dollars left.

7.

8.

NAME ___________________

Final Test Chapters 1–13

Round each number to the place named.

	a	b	c	d
9.	4,932 tens	59,651 hundreds	596 hundreds	720 hundreds
	______	______	______	______

Write each number in expanded form.

	a	b	c	d
10.	593	400,430	50,603	5,964
	______	______	______	______

Compare each pair of numbers. Write <, >, or =.

	a	b	c	d
11.	5 ___ 7	4 ___ 4	21 ___ 27	154 ___ 151

Multiply or divide.

	a	b	c	d	e
12.	3×4	52×5	42×3	7×8	61×2
13.	54×3	92×1	13×5	4×5	16×3
14.	$8\overline{)64}$	$6\overline{)24}$	$9\overline{)54}$	$4\overline{)12}$	$5\overline{)5}$
15.	$7\overline{)21}$	$4\overline{)20}$	$3\overline{)6}$	$6\overline{)18}$	$2\overline{)10}$

NAME ____________________

Final Test Chapters 1–13

SHOW YOUR WORK

Solve each problem.

16. There are 27 students in the classroom. Each math student receives 3 papers. How many total papers are there?

There are a total of __________ papers.

17. There are 64 seats in the movie theater. There are 8 rows. If the same number of seats are in each row, how many seats are in each row?

There are __________ seats in each row.

16.

17.

What fraction of each figure or set is shaded?

18.

a 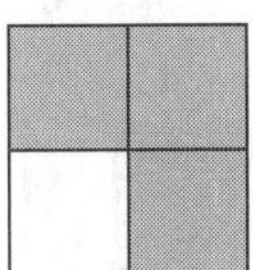 ________

b 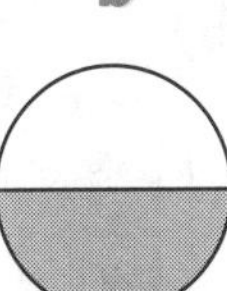 ________

c 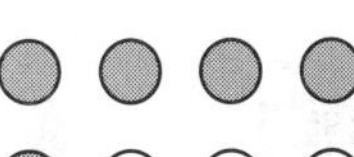 ________

d 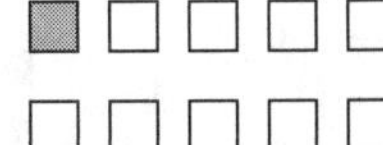 ________

What fraction of each figure is shaded? Compare the fractions. Use >, <, or =.

19.

a 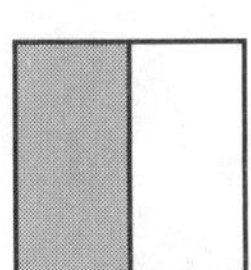

b 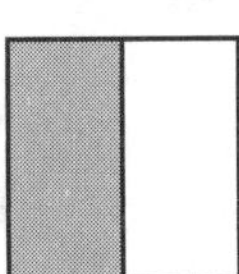 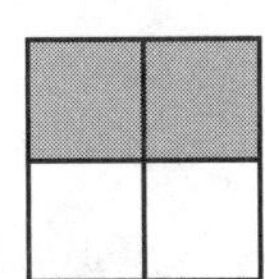

c 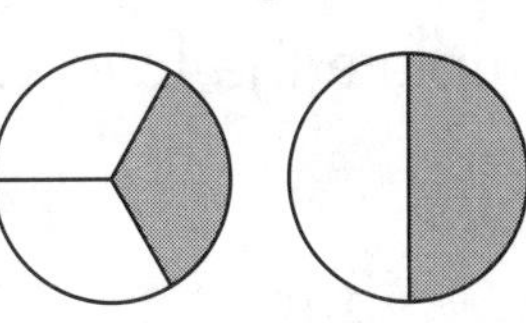

20.

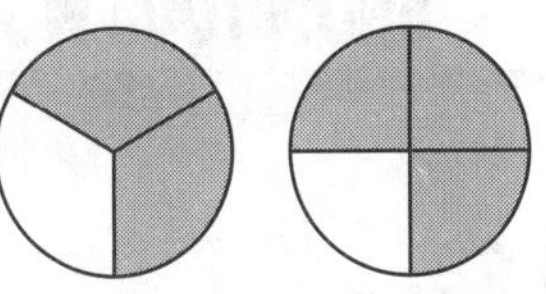

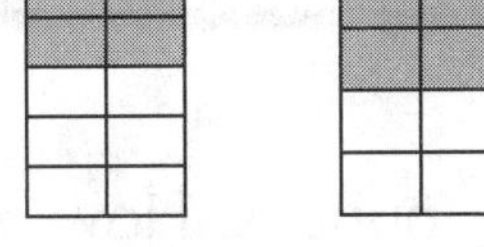

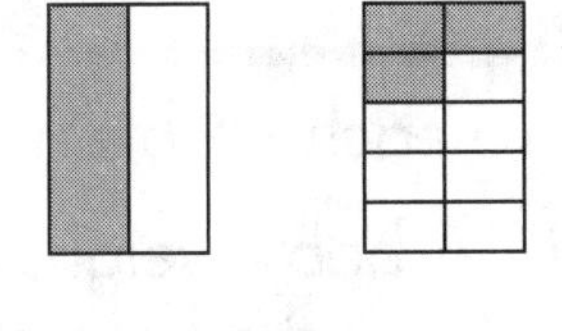

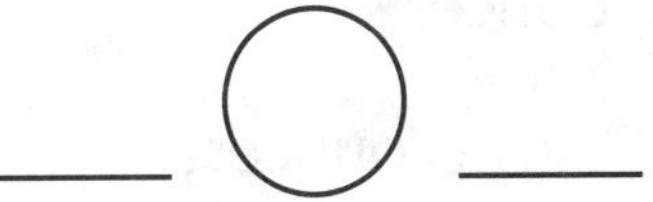

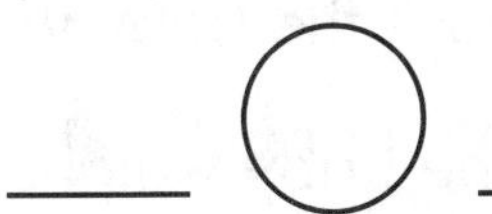

NAME ____________________

Final Test Chapters 1–13

Use a ruler to find the measure of each rectangle.

21. Measure to the nearest inch. ______ in.

22. Measure to the nearest centimeter. ______ cm

Complete the following.

	a	b	c
23.	500 cm = ______ m	5,000 g = ______ kg	6,000 mg = ______ g
24.	6,000 mL = ______ L	3 g = ______ mg	7 m = ______ cm

What is the temperature reading on each thermometer?

25.

a

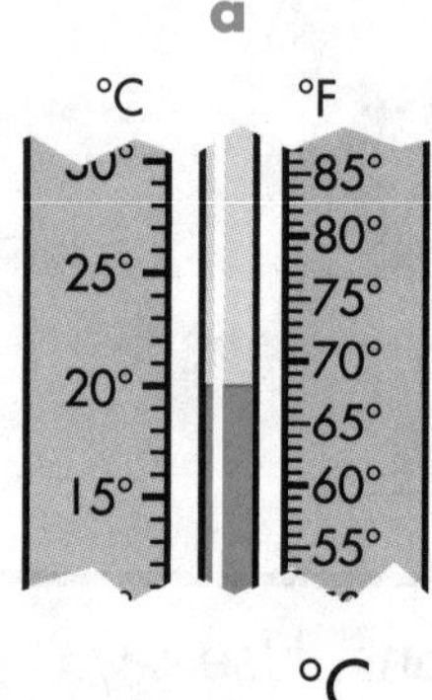

______ °C

b

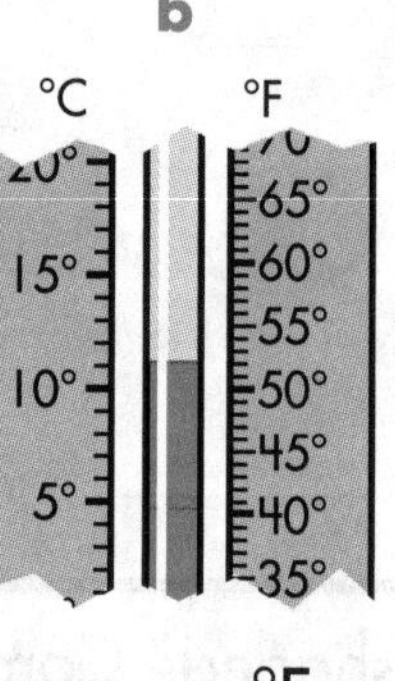

______ °F

c

______ °C ______ °F

Complete the following.

	a	b	c	d
26.	3 ft. = ___ in.	2 yd. = ___ ft.	4 c. = ___ pt.	16 pt. = ___ gal.
27.	5 gal. = ___ qt.	12 c. = ___ qt.	2 pt. = ___ c.	2 ft. = ___ in.

SHOW YOUR WORK

Solve each problem.

28. A baby weighs 5 pounds 2 ounces. How much does the baby weigh in ounces?

The baby weighs __________ ounces.

28.

NAME ______________________

Final Test Chapters 1–13

Complete the following.

29. 15 pennies have a value of ________ cents or ________ nickels.

30. 75 pennies have a value of ________ cents or ________ quarters.

31. $7.52 means ________ dollars and ________ cents.

Determine the change for the following.

32. A radio costs $5.72.

money value	$ ________
cost of radio	− ________
change	$ ________

Complete the following.

	a	b
33.	7:42 means ____ minutes after ____.	7:42 means ____ minutes to ____.

Write the time to the nearest hour, half hour, quarter hour, or minute as indicated.

34.

a	b	c	d
hour	half hour	quarter hour	minute
___ : ___	___ : ___	___ : ___	___ : ___

heads	● ● ● ● ● ◖
tails	● ● ● ●

Key: ● = 2 students

Use this picture graph to answer the following questions.

35. How many students had heads? ______

36. How many students had tails? ______

Students' Favorite Pet

Number of Students: 2, 4, 6, 8, 10, 12, 14, 16

Fish, Dog, Cat, Rabbit

Type of Pet

Use this bar graph to answer the following questions.

37. Which pet did the most students choose? ______

38. Which pet did the fewest students choose? ______

NAME ____________________

Final Test Chapters 1–13

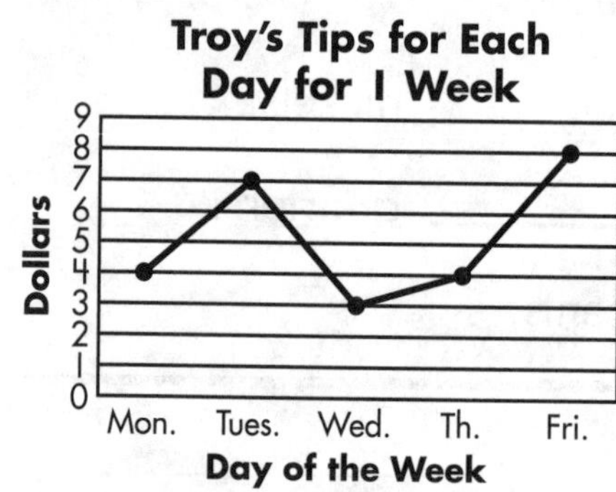

Use the line graph to answer questions 39–41.

39. What day of the week did Troy receive the most tips? ________

40. Troy received exactly 4 dollars on which days? ________

41. What is the total amount of tips that Troy received for the week? ________

Name each figure. Label each as solid or plane.

	a	b	c	d
42.	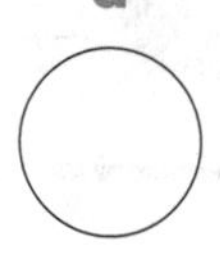			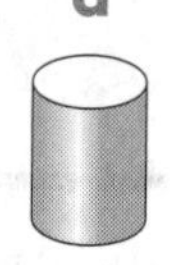
	________	________	________	________
	________	________	________	________

Name each figure.

	a	b	c	d
43.				
	________	________	________	________

Complete the pattern.

44. 20 25 30 a ___ b ___ 13 11 9 c ___ d ___

Complete the following.

	a	b	c	d
45.	$3 + 0 = \square$	$5 \times 1 = \square$	$5 + 3 = \square + 5$	$7 \times 2 = 2 \times \square$

Write the number sentence. For the missing part, use a box ($\square$). Solve each number sentence.

46. The sum of five plus two is what number? ________

The sum of five and two is ________.

NAME ______________________ DATE __________

Scoring Record for Posttests, Mid-Test, and Final Test

		Performance			
Chapter Posttest	Your Score	Excellent	Very Good	Fair	Needs Improvement
1	____ of 54	51–54	44–50	33–43	32 or fewer
2	____ of 43	41–43	35–40	27–34	26 or fewer
3	____ of 54	51–54	44–50	33–43	32 or fewer
4	____ of 45	43–45	37–42	28–36	27 or fewer
5	____ of 59	56–59	48–55	36–47	35 or fewer
6	____ of 51	48–51	42–47	32–41	31 or fewer
7	____ of 24	23–24	20–22	16–19	15 or fewer
8	____ of 15	15	13–14	10–12	9 or fewer
9	____ of 34	33–34	28–32	21–27	20 or fewer
10	____ of 46	44–46	38–43	29–37	28 or fewer
11	____ of 25	24–25	21–23	16–20	15 or fewer
12	____ of 52	49–52	43–48	32–42	31 or fewer
13	____ of 63	60–63	51–59	39–50	38 or fewer
Mid-Test	____ of 121	114–121	98–113	74–97	73 or fewer
Final Test	____ of 155	145–155	125–144	94–124	93 or fewer

Record your test score in the Your Score column. See where your score falls in the Performance columns. Your score is based on the total number of required responses. If your score is fair or needs improvement, review the chapter material.

Grade 3 Answers

Chapter 1

Pretest, page 1

	a	b	c	d	e
1.	42	22	79	86	90
2.	19	94	57	81	70
3.	53	32	45	43	95
4.	99	94	53	93	88
5.	80	7	5	20	8
6.	41	61	5	20	43
7.	39	23	54	35	65
8.	8	61	35	50	15

Pretest, page 2

9. 63; 27; 36 **10.** 43; 13; 16; 72
11. 36; 22; 14 **12.** 25

Lesson 1.1, page 3

	a	b	c	d	e	f
1.	5	16	7	8	3	14
2.	9	6	9	11	7	13
3.	7	11	14	11	14	6
4.	0	11	14	7	8	12
5.	7	4	6	10	16	9
6.	10	5	10	15	18	12

Lesson 1.2, page 4

	a	b	c	d	e	f
1.	5	6	1	5	7	5
2.	3	3	3	8	9	2
3.	5	3	6	3	7	7
4.	4	1	6	8	5	4
5.	7	2	1	9	4	6
6.	2	1	8	4	1	6

Lesson 1.3, page 5

	a	b	c	d	e	f
1.	39	33	30	28	88	76
2.	27	48	27	83	92	55
3.	26	47	59	80	77	44
4.	59	55	56	48	69	69
5.	27	58	65	93	97	58
6.	53	93	99	65	68	77

Lesson 1.4, page 6

	a	b	c	d	e	f
1.	11	64	22	20	81	32
2.	52	70	21	42	12	56
3.	41	22	27	13	44	30
4.	41	21	12	22	21	12
5.	30	21	11	54	21	16
6.	10	16	23	31	61	41

Lesson 1.5, page 7

	a	b	c	d	e	f
1.	41	91	90	52	81	48
2.	63	91	64	80	83	72
3.	81	81	45	32	56	70
4.	81	45	81	31	90	54
5.	80	45	41	52	54	91
6.	46	61	70	51	60	91

Lesson 1.6, page 8

	a	b	c	d	e	f
1.	8	3	25	14	36	59
2.	17	6	34	19	17	19
3.	35	15	46	29	25	24
4.	7	40	59	67	35	19
5.	48	27	23	57	36	19
6.	36	47	68	55	18	39

Lesson 1.7, page 9

	a	b	c	d	e	f
1.	84	92	64	68	48	90
2.	98	72	60	53	71	84
3.	83	52	19	91	74	85
4.	96	92	93	66	91	89
5.	95	68	91	55	58	75

Lesson 1.8, page 10

	a	b	c	d	e	f
1.	13	97	63	36	51	46
2.	70	17	52	33	42	13
3.	84	79	75	87	8	72
4.	67	93	14	23	40	47
5.	14	18	30	19	73	71
6.	2	61	99	56	13	91

Lesson 1.9, page 11

1. 52; 39; 91 **2.** 3; 23; 2; 28
3. 27; 31; 58 **4.** 53 **5.** 90

Lesson 1.10, page 12

1. 32; 14; 18 **2.** 15; 11; 4 **3.** 76; 62; 14
4. 17 **5.** 26

Posttest, page 13

	a	b	c	d	e	f
1.	70	39	71	33	80	27
2.	98	92	50	70	48	84
3.	60	36	20	75	77	99
4.	91	81	48	90	66	59
5.	88	63	37	26	2	63
6.	68	15	23	22	49	14
7.	23	60	56	47	64	67
8.	8	16	72	45	40	25

Grade 3 Answers

Posttest, page 14

9. 17 **10.** 38 **11.** 19 **12.** 16 **13.** 8 **14.** 17

Chapter 2

Pretest, page 15

	a	b	c	d
1.	5	5,000	500	5
2.	5,000	500,000	500	50
3.	6	2	5	6
4.	5	0	6	4

5a. 500 + 90 + 6 **5b.** 40,000 + 300 + 20 + 1
5c. 100,000 + 70,000 + 10 + 8
5d. 90,000 + 400 + 30 + 1
6a. 70 + 3 **6b.** 900 + 80 + 7
6c. 5,000 + 40 + 1
6d. 800,000 + 3,000 + 700 + 30 + 1

Pretest, page 16

	a	b	c	d
7.	30 < 32	9 < 10	171 < 1,710	596 > 593
8.	43 > 27	30 = 30	16 > 13	960 > 431
9.	96	21	460	57
10.	540	900	480	960
11.	6,000	9,650	7,400	1,610

12. 9,851 **13.** 2,237 **14.** Rick

Lesson 2.1, page 17

	a	b	c	d
1.	300	30	30	3
2.	200	3	20	20
3.	90	2	20	300

4a. 500 + 60 + 3 **4b.** 90 + 2
4c. 800 + 60 + 1 **4d.** 100 + 50 + 3
5a. 200 + 50 + 2 **5b.** 10 + 8
5c. 60 + 5 **5d.** 300 + 90 + 2

Lesson 2.1, page 18

1. 200 + 10 + 3 **2.** 3 ; 2 ; 5
3. $200; $30; 0; 0; $230 **4.** 60; 6; 657

Lesson 2.2, page 19

	a	b	c	d
1.	5,000	50,000	5	50
2.	2	9	3	6

3a. 3; ten thousands **3b.** 4; hundreds
3c. 2; thousands **3d.** 6; hundreds
4a. 50,000 + 600 + 30 + 1
4b. 10,000 + 2,000 + 500 + 60
4c. 900 + 60 + 3
4d. 40,000 + 3,000 + 500 + 60 + 1
5a. 80,000 + 1,000 + 9
5b. 30,000 + 2,000 + 400 + 50 + 1
5c. 6,000 + 300 + 20 **5d.** 2,000 + 400 + 6

Lesson 2.2, page 20

1. hundreds; tens; ones **2.** 8; 9; 4; 8; 5; 89,485
3. 1 ten-thousands ; 9 ones ; 12,569 **4.** 30,203

Lesson 2.3, page 21

	a	b	c	d
1.	200,000	20,000	200	2
2.	5	4	2	2

3a. 4; hundred thousands **3b.** 6; thousands
3c. 0; ten thousands **3d.** 2; thousands
4a. 600,000 + 900 + 80 + 1
4b. 700,000 + 30,000 + 100 + 4
4c. 80,000 + 300 + 60
4d. 90,000 + 1,000 + 100 + 20 + 3
5a. 100,000 + 20,000 + 3,000 + 400 + 50 + 6
5b. 90,000 + 8,000 + 700 + 30 + 1
5c. 100,000 + 3,000 + 400 + 7
5d. 600,000 + 5,000 + 400 + 30 + 1

Lesson 2.3, page 22

1. 600,903
2. 2; 5; 2; 9; 5; 5
200,000 + 50,000 + 2,000 + 900 + 50 + 5
3. 975,321 **4.** 123,579

Lesson 2.4, page 23

1a. 3,342 > 3,339 **1b.** 305 > 272
1c. 200 = 200 **1d.** 180 < 810
2a. 352 < 357 **2b.** 75 > 70
2c. 186 < 286 **2d.** 910 = 910
3a. 1,964 > 1,694 **3b.** 3,721 > 986
3c. 2,545 > 2,541 **3d.** 183 < 189

	a	b	c	d
4.	9,000	67	1,100	11
5.	27	86	80,100	323

6. Andy and Sheila **7.** Adelina

Lesson 2.5, page 24

	a	b	c	d
1.	960	150	190	4,030
2.	130	3,450	8,660	7,990
3.	8,800	1,000	3,300	7,900
4.	500	1,300	800	4,400
5.	8,600	2,000	360	1,540
6.	1,900	770	900	90
7.	450	8,710	500	5,330
8.	4,000	120	490	2,400

Posttest, page 25

	a	b	c	d
1.	2	200	200	2,000
2.	20	20	20,000	2
3.	3	1	9	6

Grade 3 Answers

4a. 5; thousands **4b.** 0; tens
4c. 8; hundreds **4d.** 7; ones
5a. 500 + 90 + 2 **5b.** 4,000 + 500 + 30 + 2
5c. 4,000 + 900 + 7
5d. 10,000 + 6,000 + 900 + 80 + 3
6a. 10,000 + 700
6b. 100,000 + 80,000 + 900 + 80 + 2
6c. 90,000 + 500 + 30 + 1 **6d.** 60 + 3

Posttest, page 26

7a. 52 < 96 **7b.** 5 < 8
7c. 73 > 72 **7d.** 980 > 970

	a	b	c	d
8.	17	32	760	102
9.	21	56	20	14
10.	600	90	5,000	980

11. 76,430 **12.** 4,030 **13.** 40

Chapter 3

Pretest, page 27

	a	b	c	d	e	f
1.	70	178	182	95	199	283
2.	792	979	420	905	369	160
3.	228	277	208	169	77	417
4.	80	121	818	967	599	68
5.	108	64	510	16	94	639
6.	444	442	848	602	732	40
7.	35	52	37	61	609	426
8.	810	44	65	430	534	137

Pretest, page 28

9. subtract; 14 **10.** add; 81 **11.** add; 73
12. 107 **13.** 204

Lesson 3.1, page 29

	a	b	c	d	e	f
1.	118	103	140	118	110	162
2.	94	119	105	113	158	114
3.	102	119	161	115	127	121
4.	114	104	119	102	105	170
5.	100	107	120	111	139	86
6.	139	187	150	118	126	139

Lesson 3.1, page 30

1. 58; 47; 105 **2.** 72; 43; 115
3. 92; 87; 179 **4.** 77; 52; 129

Lesson 3.2, page 31

	a	b	c	d	e	f
1.	140	61	151	111	94	92
2.	81	110	104	111	121	145
3.	141	44	120	93	91	111
4.	81	134	121	94	62	80
5.	43	101	80	141	127	92
6.	114	122	120	94	88	77
7.	93	124	92	70	122	71

Lesson 3.2, page 32

	a	b	c	d	e	f
1.	89	78	88	86	77	39
2.	79	79	67	66	68	86
3.	26	8	48	89	69	88
4.	78	58	69	86	59	76
5.	28	58	29	58	74	87
6.	85	69	79	75	87	58
7.	79	89	57	88	78	87

Lesson 3.2, page 33

	a	b	c	d	e	f
1.	61	109	106	92	90	31
2.	55	71	84	59	117	111
3.	80	70	105	47	74	78
4.	91	91	97	66	72	81
5.	91	67	129	85	89	89
6.	87	89	101	98	71	113
7.	58	91	116	82	79	94
8.	84	64	122	115	124	87
9.	7	78	78	49	91	87

Lesson 3.2, page 34

1. 119; 57; 62 **2.** 162; 54; 108
3. 117; 59; 58 **4.** 153; 62; 91

Lesson 3.3, page 35

	a	b	c	d	e	f
1.	685	1,153	933	1,123	444	1,656
2.	1,175	1,030	1,570	1,042	1,280	868
3.	1,282	1,001	681	973	1,356	1,194
4.	982	944	367	404	414	1,234
5.	1,424	850	1,378	1,350	446	812
6.	1,334	1,070	880	1,251	1,125	839
7.	465	922	1,334	521	967	874

Lesson 3.3, page 36

1. 232; 179; 411 **2.** 543; 476; 1,019
3. 639; 722; 1,361 **4.** 324; 187; 511

Lesson 3.4, page 37

	a	b	c	d	e	f
1.	212	593	489	120	480	148
2.	408	206	279	106	377	190
3.	331	399	519	189	577	321
4.	114	208	529	171	448	220
5.	86	627	25	350	86	838
6.	281	349	225	336	129	485

Grade 3 Answers

Lesson 3.4, page 38

1. 990; 587; 403 **2.** 530; 147; 383
3. 600; 230; 370 **4.** 171 **5.** 197

Lesson 3.5, page 39

	a	b	c	d	e	f
1.	369	901	417	732	521	290
2.	1,108	606	1,075	1,005	397	476
3.	847	711	931	550	531	506
4.	1,055	589	812	902	382	695

Lesson 3.6, page 40

	a	b	c	d	e	f
1.	570	238	33	326	165	222
2.	121	15	226	112	129	296
3.	399	220	106	263	264	405
4.	187	462	437	303	215	198

Lesson 3.7, page 41

	a	b	c	d	e	f
1.	131	179	91	94	422	214
2.	268	62	337	60	779	60
3.	447	77	89	175	198	99
4.	1,403	313	860	79	465	769
5.	905	365	370	198	204	915
6.	223	922	689	396	302	93
7.	75	119	120	649	905	293
8.	106	585	349	91	402	344
9.	1,344	118	390	580	149	628

Lesson 3.8, page 42

	a	b	c	d	e	f
1.	131	158	86	117	664	640
2.	401	162	520	140	197	102
3.	1,111	164	620	999	329	716
4.	397	108	183	409	889	105
5.	88	147	591	430	406	206
6.	306	463	378	106	403	631
7.	677	728	582	928	272	142
8.	256	459	93	452	96	930
9.	340	120	455	241	239	243

Posttest, page 43

	a	b	c	d	e	f
1.	167	345	249	402	922	868
2.	279	375	1750	345	1,273	360
3.	969	407	856	1,042	915	990
4.	829	715	1029	527	725	1,010
5.	137	106	78	40	270	186
6.	288	617	231	115	394	364
7.	159	477	187	683	485	169
8.	310	335	224	478	341	107

Posttest, page 44

9. 6 **10.** 8 **11.** 219 **12.** 1,223 **13.** 28
14. 76

Chapter 4

Pretest, page 45

	a	b	c	d	e
1.	39	162	62	22	126
2.	961	730	1308	1444	1691
3.	6556	9315	6796	7162	9971
4.	4197	4200	5371	3611	8239
5.	960	1540	380	3340	3881
6.	1675	3811	733	1117	830
7.	2822	292	391	300	3780
8.	131	1910	5760	3279	611

Pretest, page 46

9. 11 **10.** 205 **11.** 37 **12.** 63 **13.** 1759
14. 2,802

Lesson 4.1, page 47

	a	b	c	d	e	f
1.	18	20	31	44	97	16
2.	133	153	123	83	142	150
3.	251	120	120	223	157	55
4.	163	183	188	39	120	212
5.	224	202	215	73	181	202

Lesson 4.1, page 48

1. 23; 16; 14; 7; 60 **2.** 9; 6; 7; 22
3. 53; 44; 18; 115 **4.** 25

Lesson 4.2, page 49

	a	b	c	d	e	f
1.	1,040	1,594	650	1,794	1,616	914
2.	1,612	973	2,417	445	1,100	723
3.	2,027	2,158	1,489	1,673	1,239	1,867
4.	660	1,612	1,285	1,279	1,802	1,353
5.	2,533	1,487	1,980	525	1,774	2,280

Lesson 4.2, page 50

1. 135; 213; 159; 507 **2.** 186; 175; 182; 543
3. 2,325 **4.** 442

Lesson 4.3, page 51

	a	b	c	d	e	f
1.	9,057	9,873	7,389	7,464	9,469	9,803
2.	3,764	9,990	9,311	7,296	9,793	8,052
3.	7,757	9,281	8,405	4,065	9,173	8,485
4.	8,420	9,465	3,578	8,874	9,717	9,512
5.	7,413	9,232	5,532	9,044	9,768	6,708
6.	7,437	7,309	6,858	9,914	9,292	9,905

Grade 3 Answers

Lesson 4.3, page 52

1. 1,523; 1,695; 3,218 **2.** 1,200; 1,320; 2,520
3. 2,122 **4.** 2,600

Lesson 4.4, page 53

	a	b	c	d	e
1.	7483	6736	4661	1742	894
2.	1882	8080	6982	7882	3872
3.	4092	595	1582	5291	7481
4.	6891	2795	7492	3493	2791
5.	8891	2893	1781	2892	7641
6.	4672	3480	6891	3294	4573

Lesson 4.4, page 54

1. 2,532; 1,341; 1,191 **2.** 1,250; 495; 755
3. 1,986; 103; 1,883 **4.** 54 **5.** 191

Lesson 4.5, page 55

	a	b	c	d
1.	70	30	110	130
2.	140	170	260	250
3.	500	500	1100	800
4.	1500	1600	6200	5300
5.	5000	1300	12000	5000

Lesson 4.5, page 56

1. 900 **2.** 30 **3.** 800 **4.** 130 **5.** 500

Lesson 4.6, page 57

	a	b	c	d
1.	20	40	10	30
2.	380	930	730	480
3.	200	400	300	500
4.	800	2400	4100	7000
5.	5000	6000	1000	8000

Lesson 4.6, page 58

1. 20 **2.** 100 **3.** 200 **4.** 110 **5.** 110

Posttest, page 59

	a	b	c	d	e
1.	63	89	153	102	189
2.	742	630	531	712	902
3.	6293	6348	9256	6553	7974
4.	6306	5307	7031	4875	4605
5.	2891	2041	5080	1771	5092
6.	1791	4490	7171	4194	392
7.	6506	3192	2882	2891	1884
8.	3891	4285	3387	2090	7691

Posttest, page 60

9. 115 **10.** 1894 **11.** 110 **12.** 1000 **13.** 30

Chapter 5

Pretest, page 61

	a	b	c	d	e	f
1.	0	5	12	0	30	24
2.	14	27	64	18	20	20
3.	36	27	7	15	12	4
4.	0	28	54	16	5	18
5.	28	21	6	8	9	30
6.	80	42	87	128	192	81
7.	184	72	183	140	208	65
8.	105	45	124	180	168	129
9.	54	88	62	270	59	60

Pretest, page 62

10. 92 **11.** 65 **12.** 15 **13.** 40 **14.** 75

Lesson 5.1, page 63

	a	b	c	d	e
1.	6	14	12	18	16
2.	4	2	15	18	9
3.	6	3	12	21	8
4.	16	4	20	36	32
5.	12	8	10	24	27
6.	24	28	6	21	18

Lesson 5.2, page 64

	a	b	c	d	e	f
1.	0	27	30	4	5	18
2.	18	40	40	0	18	12
3.	24	21	6	14	15	4
4.	12	25	9	8	21	0
5.	0	18	35	30	6	8
6.	28	9	9	14	0	3

Lesson 5.3, page 65

	a	b	c	d	e	f
1.	27	42	20	63	48	0
2.	12	40	36	0	35	18
3.	5	24	16	48	0	0
4.	3	24	18	12	18	30
5.	24	18	42	81	32	15
6.	12	64	27	28	0	49

Lesson 5.3, page 66

1. 6; 5; 30 **2.** 7; 9; 63
3. 4; 8; 32 **4.** 20 **5.** 16

Lesson 5.4, page 67

	a	b	c	d	e	f
1.	146	28	450	45	99	186
2.	88	86	208	155	46	128
3.	19	84	129	27	455	166
4.	56	104	189	73	124	35

Grade 3 Answers

Lesson 5.4, page 68

	a	b	c	d	e	f
1.	155	84	36	208	249	75
2.	39	164	104	28	39	150
3.	108	17	0	69	168	205
4.	305	216	28	86	47	276
5.	166	126	207	55	122	58
6.	26	50	46	42	328	124
7.	66	66	129	156	184	54

Lesson 5.5, page 69

	a	b	c	d	e	f
1.	74	95	90	76	75	60
2.	56	94	84	52	92	96
3.	52	72	65	45	54	90
4.	75	51	72	78	70	32
5.	81	60	58	78	72	85
6.	70	50	56	42	68	87

Lesson 5.5, page 70

	a	b	c	d	e	f
1.	360	152	145	108	125	144
2.	162	288	336	460	141	172
3.	135	115	258	365	110	224
4.	192	372	430	172	114	296
5.	102	140	111	184	115	332
6.	132	177	410	370	252	188

Lesson 5.6, page 71

	a	b	c	d	e	f
1.	65	14	0	324	84	52
2.	156	380	205	6	42	85
3.	225	279	126	66	50	32
4.	102	91	85	62	125	120
5.	160	56	45	0	38	288
6.	54	28	22	57	166	270
7.	30	159	72	48	26	68
8.	28	0	6	16	112	57
9.	138	129	54	90	20	39

Lesson 5.6, page 72

1. 56; 3; 168 **2.** 32; 5; 160
3. 24; 4; 96 **4.** 22 **5.** 72

Posttest, page 73

	a	b	c	d	e	f
1.	5	81	6	20	18	0
2.	63	10	6	16	35	12
3.	30	24	12	0	12	28
4.	26	92	85	42	0	0
5.	108	192	159	66	55	120
6.	142	54	100	42	27	38
7.	87	270	84	92	65	36
8.	80	186	68	45	93	63
9.	66	126	44	160	90	475

Posttest, page 74

10. 15 **11.** 116 **12.** 150 **13.** 14 **14.** 132

Chapter 6

Pretest, page 75

	a	b	c	d	e
1.	9	9	2	2	6
2.	3	9	1	5	3
3.	2	7	8	8	4
4.	5	2	2	3	6
5.	7	7	8	7	8
6.	4	8	1	9	7
7.	5	3	5	6	8
8.	9	5	2	4	6
9.	1	4	4	5	8

Pretest, page 76

10. 9 **11.** 6 **12.** 8 **13.** 3 **14.** 2 **15.** 9

Lesson 6.1, page 77

1. 12; 2 **2.** 24; 3 **3.** 36; 9 **4.** 4; 8; 2
5. 7; 35; 5 **6.** 20; 4 **7.** 27; 3
8. 6; 3 **9.** 3; 15; 5 **10.** 2 ; 14 ; 7

Lesson 6.1, page 78

1a. 4; 4; $4 \times 3 = 12$ **1b.** 3; 3; $3 \times 4 = 12$
2a. 4; 5; 5; $5 \times 4 = 20$ **2b.** 5; 4; 4; $4 \times 5 = 20$
3a. 12; 2; 6; 6; $6 \times 2 = 12$
3b. 12; 6; 2; 2; $2 \times 6 = 12$

Lesson 6.2, page 79

1a. 2; $3 \times 2 = 6$ **1b.** 7; $2 \times 7 = 14$
1c. 5; $1 \times 5 = 5$ **1d.** 2; $2 \times 2 = 4$
1e. 4; $1 \times 4 = 4$
2a. 9; $3 \times 9 = 27$ **2b.** 3; $1 \times 3 = 3$
2c. 9; $2 \times 9 = 18$ **2d.** 7; $1 \times 7 = 7$
2e. 7; $3 \times 7 = 21$
3a. 4; $3 \times 4 = 12$ **3b.** 8; $2 \times 8 = 16$
3c. 5; $1 \times 5 = 5$ **3d.** 6; $3 \times 6 = 18$
3e. 5; $2 \times 5 = 10$
4a. 6; $1 \times 6 = 6$ **4b.** 8; $1 \times 8 = 8$
4c. 4; $2 \times 4 = 8$ **4d.** 2; $1 \times 2 = 2$
4e. 1; $1 \times 1 = 1$
5a. 8; $3 \times 8 = 24$ **5b.** 3; $3 \times 3 = 9$
5c. 9; $1 \times 9 = 9$ **5d.** 3; $2 \times 3 = 6$
5e. 1; $2 \times 1 = 2$

Lesson 6.2, page 80

1. 18; 3; 6 **2.** 16; 2; 8 **3.** 12; 2; 6
4. 5 **5.** 9

Lesson 6.3, page 81

1a. 9 ; $6 \times 9 = 54$ **1b.** 9 ; $3 \times 9 = 27$
1c. 8 ; $6 \times 8 = 48$ **1d.** 5 ; $5 \times 5 = 25$
1e. 9 ; $4 \times 9 = 36$
2a. 6 ; $5 \times 6 = 30$ **2b.** 6 ; $4 \times 6 = 24$
2c. 8 ; $4 \times 8 = 32$ **2d.** 4 ; $4 \times 4 = 16$
2e. 5 ; $4 \times 5 = 20$

	a	b	c	d	e
3.	6	7	7	4	7
4.	9	2	8	8	3
5.	4	8	3	9	3
6.	3	7	6	1	9

Lesson 6.3, page 82

1. 24; 6; 4 **2.** 30; 6; 5 **3.** 42; 6; 7
4. 3 **5.** 8

Lesson 6.4, page 83

1a. 1; $7 \times 1 = 7$ **1b.** 4; $6 \times 4 = 24$
1c. 7; $8 \times 7 = 56$ **1d.** 5; $6 \times 5 = 30$
1e. 8; $8 \times 8 = 64$
2a. 2; $6 \times 2 = 12$ **2b.** 5; $7 \times 5 = 35$
2c. 3; $8 \times 3 = 24$ **2d.** 4; $7 \times 4 = 28$
2e. 6; $6 \times 6 = 36$

	a	b	c	d	e
3.	7	9	8	7	3
4.	2	2	3	6	5
5.	7	2	3	1	6
6.	3	6	1	9	5

Lesson 6.4, page 84

1. 72; 9; 8 **2.** 40; 8; 5 **3.** 16; 8; 2 **4.** 9

Lesson 6.5, page 85

	a	b	c	d	e
1.	5	4	3	9	3
2.	9	9	8	7	1
3.	8	7	4	7	9
4.	2	2	5	3	3
5.	6	5	1	9	3
6.	4	9	4	6	9
7.	1	8	6	9	8
8.	6	5	7	6	5
9.	3	4	9	2	1
10.	7	7	9	2	7

Lesson 6.6, page 86

	a	b	c	d	e	f
1.	2	2	9	9	9	2
2.	5	6	3	3	8	4
3.	8	3	4	7	1	6
4.	6	2	9	1	4	5
5.	2	5	5	8	4	7
6.	258	360	268	819	154	60
7.	102	266	344	29	108	291
8.	42	144	410	99	136	112
9.	78	70	365	512	279	18
10.	424	304	147	178	235	252

Posttest, page 87

	a	b	c	d	e
1.	4	8	7	6	4
2.	6	1	3	6	4
3.	2	5	6	2	2
4.	1	5	3	9	3
5.	7	5	3	5	6
6.	9	3	8	8	8
7.	9	4	4	6	4
8.	1	3	9	1	8
9.	7	7	6	8	7

Posttest, page 88

10. 8 **11.** 6 **12.** 5 **13.** 4 **14.** 9 **15.** 5

Mid-Test

page 89

	a	b	c	d	e
1.	8	19	35	26	26
2.	67	58	135	70	150
3.	139	140	719	1008	1113
4.	104	115	70	983	1656
5.	40	26	7	8	16
6.	17	9	71	59	19
7.	480	114	513	541	711
8.	100	111	191	376	104

page 90

	a	b	c	d	e
9.	1,345	9,516	8,454	8,665	7,834
10.	9,093	7,372	6,963	4,512	8,993
11.	4,900	8,241	5,352	1,101	2,000
12.	4,786	6,990	2,091	7,881	4,891
13.	5,430	990	78,700	9,870	54,000

14a. 50,000 + 400 + 60 + 2
14b. 10,000 + 9,000 + 700 + 80 + 3
14c. 500 + 40 + 3 **14d.** 10,000 + 30
15a. $32 < 93$ **15b.** $110 = 110$
15c. $54 > 52$ **15d.** $16 < 61$ **15e.** $103 > 13$

page 91

	a	b	c	d	e
16.	25	6	145	56	18
17.	252	63	30	88	39
18.	42	51	170	106	72
19.	60	186	57	8	92

20.	3	6	6	2	1
21.	9	7	8	2	6
22.	2	1	2	9	3
23.	7	2	8	5	3

page 92

24. 113 **25.** 80 **26.** 271 **27.** 956 **28.** 1,889
29. 28 **30.** 5

Chapter 7

Pretest, page 93

	a	b	c
1.	$\frac{2}{3}$	$\frac{1}{4}$	$\frac{2}{5}$
2.	$\frac{2}{4}$	$\frac{6}{8}$	$\frac{5}{8}$
3.	$\frac{1}{5}$	$\frac{1}{4}$	$\frac{3}{10}$
4.	$\frac{5}{10}$	$\frac{1}{2}$	$\frac{3}{4}$

Pretest, page 94

	a	b	c
5.	$\frac{1}{2} > \frac{1}{4}$	$\frac{1}{5} < \frac{2}{5}$	$\frac{1}{4} < \frac{1}{3}$
6.	$\frac{5}{8} > \frac{1}{4}$	$\frac{2}{3} < \frac{3}{4}$	$\frac{1}{5} = \frac{2}{10}$
7.	$\frac{3}{4} > \frac{1}{2}$	$\frac{4}{5} < \frac{9}{10}$	$\frac{5}{8} < \frac{3}{4}$
8.	$\frac{1}{2} > \frac{1}{3}$	$\frac{4}{10} < \frac{8}{10}$	$\frac{1}{2} = \frac{2}{4}$

Lesson 7.1, page 95

	a	b	c
1.	$\frac{1}{3}$	$\frac{3}{4}$	$\frac{4}{5}$
2.	$\frac{1}{10}$	$\frac{3}{8}$	$\frac{1}{2}$
3.	$\frac{2}{3}$	$\frac{4}{8}$	$\frac{2}{5}$
4.	$\frac{2}{4}$	$\frac{3}{5}$	$\frac{4}{10}$

Lesson 7.2, page 96

	a	b	c
1.	$\frac{4}{5}$	$\frac{1}{4}$	$\frac{4}{8}$
2.	$\frac{1}{10}$	$\frac{2}{3}$	$\frac{3}{8}$
3.	$\frac{1}{2}$	$\frac{2}{5}$	$\frac{9}{10}$

	a	b	c	d
4.	▲▲△△ ▲▲△△	●● ●○	■■■□□ □□□□□	▲△△ △△

Lesson 7.3, page 97

	a	b	c
1.	$\frac{1}{4} < \frac{3}{4}$	$\frac{1}{2} = \frac{2}{4}$	$\frac{2}{3} > \frac{1}{2}$
2.	$\frac{7}{10} > \frac{3}{5}$	$\frac{3}{8} < \frac{3}{4}$	$\frac{1}{3} < \frac{5}{8}$
3.	$\frac{1}{5} = \frac{2}{10}$	$\frac{3}{4} > \frac{1}{2}$	$\frac{6}{10} > \frac{2}{5}$

Lesson 7.3, page 98

	a	b	c
1.	$\frac{1}{2} = \frac{2}{4}$	$\frac{2}{3} < \frac{3}{4}$	$\frac{1}{5} < \frac{2}{5}$
2.	$\frac{3}{4} < \frac{7}{8}$	$\frac{2}{3} > \frac{1}{4}$	$\frac{5}{8} < \frac{2}{3}$
3.	$\frac{4}{5} = \frac{8}{10}$	$\frac{1}{2} < \frac{3}{4}$	$\frac{5}{8} < \frac{8}{10}$

Posttest, page 99

	a	b	c
1.	$\frac{1}{5}$	$\frac{3}{4}$	$\frac{1}{3}$
2.	$\frac{3}{8}$	$\frac{3}{5}$	$\frac{7}{10}$
3.	$\frac{1}{4}$	$\frac{3}{8}$	$\frac{5}{10}$
4.	$\frac{3}{5}$	$\frac{1}{2}$	$\frac{7}{8}$

Posttest, page 100

	a	b	c
5.	$\frac{1}{5} < \frac{2}{5}$	$\frac{1}{3} < \frac{7}{8}$	$\frac{4}{8} = \frac{1}{2}$
6.	$\frac{1}{3} < \frac{1}{2}$	$\frac{3}{5} > \frac{2}{10}$	$\frac{4}{8} = \frac{2}{4}$
7.	$\frac{1}{2} < \frac{3}{4}$	$\frac{1}{4} > \frac{1}{8}$	$\frac{2}{3} < \frac{6}{8}$
8.	$\frac{4}{10} = \frac{2}{5}$	$\frac{2}{3} > \frac{4}{8}$	$\frac{1}{3} < \frac{3}{4}$

Chapter 8

Pretest, page 101

1. 5 in. **2.** 2 in. **3.** 1 in. **4.** 9 yd. **5.** 1 ft.
6. can **7.** has **8.** 48

Pretest, page 102

9. 2 lb. **10.** 20 ounces **11.** ounces **12.** feet
13. gallons **14.** quarts **15.** 8 pt. **16.** 13°

Lesson 8.1, page 103

1. 3 in. **2.** 2 in. **3.** 1 in. **4.** 2 in. **5.** 4 in.
6. 6 in.

Lesson 8.1, page 104

1. 1 in. **2.** 5 in. **3.** 2 in. **4.** 4 in. **5.** 3 in.
6. 2 in. **7.** 6 in.

Lesson 8.2, page 105

	a	b	c
1.	36 in.	2 ft.	144 in.
2.	1 ft.	7 yd.	6 ft.
3.	1 yd.	180 in.	216 in.
4.	15 ft.	3 ft.	12 ft.
5.	12 in.	9 ft.	2 yd.
6.	5 yd.	324 in.	108 in.
7.	2 yd.	9 yd.	24 in.
8.	72 in.	60 in.	288 in.
9.	72 in.	6 yd.	3 yd.
10.	4 yd.	48 in.	8 yd.

Grade 3 Answers

11.	84 in.	252 in.	18 ft.
12.	1 yd.	21 ft.	24 ft.

Lesson 8.3, page 106

	a	b	c
1.	4 c.	2 gal.	5 gal.
2.	3 qt.	8 qt.	8 qt.
3.	2 qt.	20 c.	8 gal.
4.	16 c.	6 pt.	1 pt.
5.	1 gal.	5 qt.	4 pt.
6.	16 pt.	4 qt.	20 c.
7.	20 qt.	6 gal.	12 c.
8.	5 gal.	7 qt.	12 qt.
9.	34 pt.	4 gal.	144 c.
10.	80 c.	5 pt.	16 pt.
11.	12 qt.	8 pt.	40 c.
12.	2 gal.	4 qt.	26 c.

Lesson 8.4, page 107

1. pound **2.** 1 pound **3.** they are the same
4. 14 ounces of cheese **5.** 5 ounces **6.** 40 pounds

	a	b	c
7.	ounce	ounce	pound
8.	ounce	ounce	ounce
9.	pound	pound	ounce
10.	pound	pound	pound

Lesson 8.5, page 108

	a	b	c
1.	20°	27°	93°
2.	35°	16°	23°
3.	62°	85°	59°

Lesson 8.6, page 109

1. 24 in. **2.** 4 ft. **3.** 2 pt. **4.** 2 qt.
5. gallons **6.** cups **7.** cold **8.** hot

Lesson 8.7, page 110

1. 46 ; 48 ; Akira **2.** 6 ft. **3.** inches **4.** yards
5. 96 oz. **6.** pounds **7.** 63° ; 32° ; 31°

Posttest, page 111

1. 4 in. **2.** 2 in. **3.** 3 in. **4.** 15 ft.
5. cannot **6.** 8 in. **7.** 20 c. **8.** 1 gal.

Posttest, page 112

9. 3-pound bag of vegetables **10.** 10 pt. **11.** 5 lb.
12. yards **13.** feet **14.** cups **15.** 54°

Chapter 9

Pretest, page 113

1. 6 cm **2.** 3 cm **3.** 8 cm

	a	b	c
4.	200 cm	5 kg	8 L
5.	5 g	1,000 mL	500 cm
6.	5,000 mL	7,000 g	7,000 mg
7.	3 m	300 cm	4 L
8.	5,000 g	2,000 mg	2 m
9.	400 cm	6 g	600 cm
10.	0°; 32°	16°; 61°	23°; 73°

Pretest, page 114

11. cannot **12.** Tina **13.** 700 mL
14. 200 mL **15.** 5,000 **16.** 6,057 g **17.** 12°

Lesson 9.1, page 115

1. 14 cm **2.** 5 cm **3.** 13 cm **4.** 10 cm
5. 6 cm **6.** 9 cm

Lesson 9.1, page 116

1. 6 cm **2.** 4 cm **3.** 11 cm

	a	b	c
4.	1,000 cm	2 m	6 m
5.	1,200 cm	300 cm	200 cm

Lesson 9.2, page 117

	a	b	c
1.	3,000 mL	2,000 mL	7 L
2.	2 L	4 L	5,000 mL

3. 500 mL **4.** 4,534 mL **5.** 500 L **6.** 300 mL

	a	b	c
7.	liters	milliliters	milliliters
8.	milliliters	liters	liters

Lesson 9.3, page 118

1. gram **2.** gram **3.** 1,000 **4.** 3

	a	b	c
5.	kg	mg	kg
6.	kg	mg	g
7.	g	g	kg
8.	mg	g	kg

Lesson 9.4, page 119

	a	b	c
1.	30°; 86°	7°; 45°	13°; 55°
2.	1°; 34°	5°; 41°	24°; 75°
3.	2°; 36°	5°; 41°	13°; 55°

Lesson 9.5, page 120

1. 10 **2.** 200 cm **3.** milliliters **4.** 3 L
5. 2 kg **6.** 2 g **7.** 10°C **8.** 23°

Posttest, page 121

1. 5 cm **2.** 12 cm **3.** 7 cm

	a	b	c
4.	3 m	5 g	4 m
5.	2 m	500 cm	600 cm
6.	3,000 mg	8 kg	5 L
7.	6 L	3 kg	700 cm
8.	7 g	4 L	2 L

Grade 3 Answers

9. 5,000 mL   7,000 mg   8,000 g
10. 13°; 55°   32°; 90°   6°; 43°

Posttest, page 122

11. 103 cm **12.** 215 cm 123 cm **13.** 700 mL
14. 2,000 mL **15.** 9,5000 g **16.** 23°

Chapter 10

Pretest, page 123

1. 30; 6 **2.** 50; 1 **3.** 3; 23 **4.** 10; 9

	a	b	c	d	e
5.	$17.43	$7.14	81¢	53¢	$42.83

	a	b
6.	$2.61	$3.50
7.	58¢	58¢

58¢ is equal to 58¢

Pretest, page 124

8. $4.77; $3.53; $1.24

	a	b
9.	32; 2	28; 3
10.	45; 3	15; 4
11.	6; 7	10; 10

	a	b	c	d
12.	2:00	1:30	1:45	1:43
13.	365	12	7	
14.	24	60	29	
15.	123	1	26	

Lesson 10.1, page 125

1. 20; 2 **2.** 50; 2 **3.** 50; 1 **4.** 100; 1
5. 25; 1 **6.** 30; 3 **7.** 17; 43 **8.** 16; 7
9. 5; 95 **10.** 3; 23 **11.** 12; 50 **12.** 9; 17

Lesson 10.2, page 126

	a	b	c	d	e
1.	$8.00	$15.28	$62.38	$11.37	$40.77
2.	$32.48	$8.34	$41.30	89¢	$38.65
3.	$24.12	$23.14	$79.00	$8.34	31¢
4.	4¢	$59.11	$24.00	$11.06	$3.61
5.	82¢	37¢	$21.14	$10.43	$26.23
6.	$4.51	$9.01	83¢	35¢	$52.12

Lesson 10.3, page 127

	a	b
1.	82¢	$4.73
2.	32¢	59¢
3.	$1.61	88¢

Lesson 10.3, page 128

1. 50¢; 50¢; 50¢ is equal to 50¢
2. 83¢; 55¢; 83¢ is greater than 55¢
3. 85¢; 95¢; 85¢ is less than 95¢
4. 76¢; 76¢; 76¢ is equal to 76¢

Lesson 10.4, page 129

1. 6.50; 4.34; 2.16 **2.** 7.95; 6.82; 1.13
3. 1.24; 1.23; 0.01 **4.** 5.28; 3.46; 1.82
5. 2.70; 2.57; 0.13

Lesson 10.5, page 130

	a	b
1.	15; 6	10; 12
2.	50; 7	10; 8
3.	45; 12	15; 1
4.	30; 1	30; 2

	a	b	c	d
5.	4:20	6:13	7:10	1:50
6.	6:45	8:09	12:30	2:23

Lesson 10.5, page 131

	a	b	c	d
1.	2:00	2:30	2:15	2:20
2.	9:00	8:30	8:30	8:36

a   b

3.  

4.  

Lesson 10.6, page 132

	a	b
1.	12	7
2.	31	28
3.	29	4
4.	7	4
5.	Saturday	4
6.	May 10	October 15

	a	b	c	d
7.	135 min.	110 min.	2 hr.	3 hr.
8.	26 hr.	53 hr.	1 day; 5 hr.	2 days

Posttest, page 133

1. 25; 1 **2.** 100; 1 **3.** 6; 19 **4.** 5; 26

	a	b	c	d	e
5.	$12.72	90¢	$64.81	$80.46	19¢

	a	b
6.	$1.88	92¢
7.	68¢	82¢

68¢ is less than 82¢

Grade 3 Answers

Posttest, page 134

8. \$4.55 ; \$3.48 ; \$1.07

	a	b	c	d
9.	15 ; 4	15 ; 8		
10.	55 ; 12	5 ; 1		
11.	23 ; 3	20 ; 7		
12.	7:00	7:30	7:15	7:18
13.	24	12	366	
14.	60	7	365	
15.	93	1	49	

Chapter 11

Pretest, page 135

1. grape **2.** apple and banana **3.** strawberry
4. 10 **5.** 9 **6.** 10 **7.** 9 **8.** white **9.** blue
10. 9 **11.** black and pink **12.** yellow

Pretest, page 136

13. August **14.** March **15.** 11
16. March **17.** April and May **18.** 3 in.
19. 2 in. **20.** $\frac{5}{8}$ **21.** $\frac{3}{8}$ **22.** $\frac{0}{8}$ **23.** likely
24. certain **25.** unlikely

Lesson 11.1, page 137

1. brown **2.** red **3.** 10 **4.** 11 **5.** brown

Lesson 11.2, page 138

1. football **2.** baseball **3.** basketball **4.** 12
5. 18 **6.** 8 **7.** 4

Lesson 11.3, page 139

1. week 5 **2.** week 3 **3.** 75 **4.** 65
5. yes, weeks 1 and 6 **6.** 2 **7.** 5

Lesson 11.4, page 140

1. $\frac{2}{2}$; certain **2.** $\frac{1}{2}$; equally likely
3. $\frac{2}{12}$; unlikely **4.** $\frac{9}{12}$; likely
5. $\frac{5}{6}$; likely

Posttest, page 141

1. May, June, October **2.** 6 **3.** 2 **4.** April
5. 4 **6.** November **7.** March and September
8. 5 **9.** brown **10.** green **11.** hazel
12. brown **13.** 2

Posttest, page 142

14. games 1 and 5 **15.** game 2 **16.** 48
17. game 2 **18.** game 3 **19.** 12 **20.** $\frac{6}{12}$ **21.** $\frac{3}{12}$
22. $\frac{3}{12}$ **23.** certain **24.** impossible **25.** likely

Chapter 12

Pretest, page 143

1. A **2.** D **3.** B **4.** C **5.** G **6.** F **7.** E

	a	b	c	d	e
8.	solid	solid	plane	solid	plane

9. 4; 4; 0 **10.** 0; 0; 0 **11.** 4; 4; 0
12. 6; 0; 0; 12 **13.** 1; 4; 0; 8 **14.** 0; 0; 0; 0

Pretest, page 144

	a	b	c	d
15.	not congruent	not congruent	congruent	congruent
16.	symmetrical	not symmetrical	not symmetrical	 symmetrical
17.	yes	no	no	yes
18.	line segment $\overline{AB}$	angle $\angle CDE$	ray $\overrightarrow{FG}$	line $\overleftrightarrow{HJ}$

Lesson 12.1, page 145

1. a triangle, b rectangle, c square, d circle

	a	b	c	d	e
2.	0	4	3	4	3
3.	0	4	1	4	0
4.	0	0	2	0	3

Lesson 12.2, page 146

1. 6; 0; 0 **2.** 0; 6; 0 **3.** 1; 0; 4 **4.** 0
5. 8 **6.** 12 **7.** 12 **8.** 5
9. Answers may vary.
10. Answers may vary.

Lesson 12.3, page 147

	a	b	c	d
1.	solid	solid	plane	plane
2.	solid	plane	plane	solid

3. B **4.** B **5.** C **6.** A **7.** D **8.** C or D

Lesson 12.4, page 148

	a	b	c	d
1.	not congruent	congruent	not congruent	not congruent
2.	not congruent	congruent	congruent	congruent
3.	congruent	not congruent	not congruent	not congruent
4.	not congruent	not congruent	congruent	congruent

Grade 3 Answers

5.	not congruent	not congruent	congruent	not congruent

Lesson 12.5, page 149

	a	b	c	d
1.	yes	no	yes	no
2.	no	yes	no	yes
3.	symmetrical	symmetrical	not symmetrical	not symmetrical
4.	not symmetrical	symmetrical	symmetrical	not symmetrical

Lesson 12.6, page 150

	a	b	c	d	e
1.	line segment $\overline{AB}$	point P	point Q	angle $\angle 3$	ray $\overrightarrow{XY}$
2.	line $\overleftrightarrow{FM}$	ray $\overrightarrow{RS}$	angle $\angle M$	angle $\angle TVW$	line $\overleftrightarrow{AB}$

3. X **4.** ray

5a. ⟷ **5b.** •——•

5c. •——→ **5d.** ∠ **5e.** •

Posttest, page 151

1a. cube; solid **1b.** triangle; plane
1c. square pyramid; solid **1d.** cylinder; solid
2a. rectangular prism; solid **2b.** triangle; plane
2c. rectangle; plane **2d.** sphere; solid
3a. cone; solid **3b.** rectangle; plane
3c. circle; plane **3d.** square; plane

	a	b	c	d
4.	4	12	4	8
5.	0	6	6	5

Posttest, page 152

	a	b	c	d
6.	congruent	congruent	not congruent	not congruent
7.	not symmetrical	symmetrical	symmetrical	not symmetrical

8. yes; yes; yes; no
9. B **10.** D **11.** A **12.** C **13.** H **14.** I
15. J **16.** G

Chapter 13

Pretest, page 153

1.

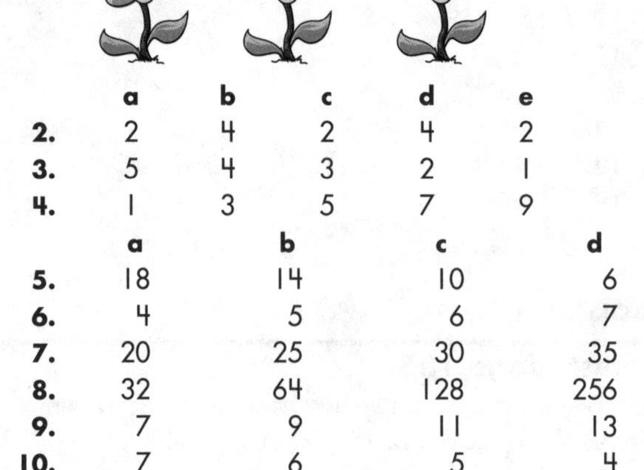

	a	b	c	d	e
2.	2	4	2	4	2
3.	5	4	3	2	1
4.	1	3	5	7	9

	a	b	c	d
5.	18	14	10	6
6.	4	5	6	7
7.	20	25	30	35
8.	32	64	128	256
9.	7	9	11	13
10.	7	6	5	4

Pretest, page 154

11. – **13.**

	a	b	c	d
14.	0	5	7	6
15.	7	5	3	2

16. 2 + 3 = □; five **17.** 5 × 4 = □; twenty
18. 10 − 8 = □; two

Lesson 13.1, page 155

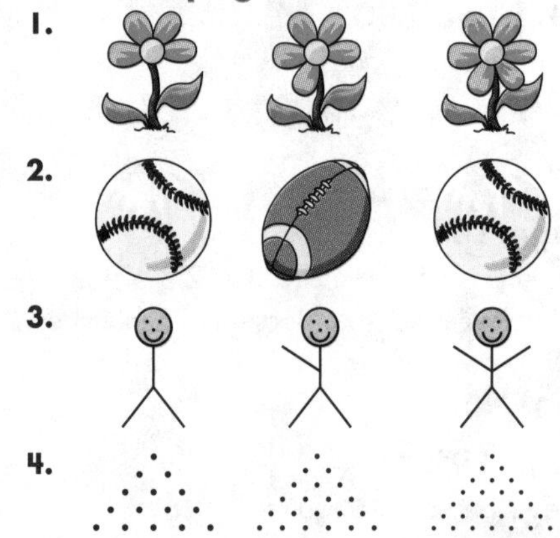

Grade 3 Answers

Lesson 13.2, page 156

	a	b	c	d	e
1.	5	4	3	2	1
2.	2	4	2	4	2
3.	1	3	5	7	9
4.	2	4	6	8	10
5.	1	2	4	8	16

Lesson 13.3, page 157

	a	b	c
1.	8	10	12
2.	7	9	11
3.	14	12	10
4.	6	3	1
5.	10	9	8
6.	20	25	30
7.	12	15	18
8.	70	110	160
9.	7	4	1
10.	7	6	5

Lesson 13.4, page 158

	a	b	c
1.			
2.			
3.			
4.			
5.			
6.			
7.			
8.			

Lesson 13.5, page 159

	a	b	c	d
1.	4	6	0	0
2.	2	5	1	1
3.	2	4	1	4
4.	5	3	5	4
5.	4	6	2	5
6.	5	5	2	6
7.	3	6	2	3

Lesson 13.5, page 160

1. 2 + 3 = □; five **2.** 7 − 2 = □; five
3. 4 × 3 = □; twelve **4.** 14 ÷ 2 = □; seven
5. 5 + □ = 7; two **6.** 13 − □ = 10; three

Posttest, page 161

1.

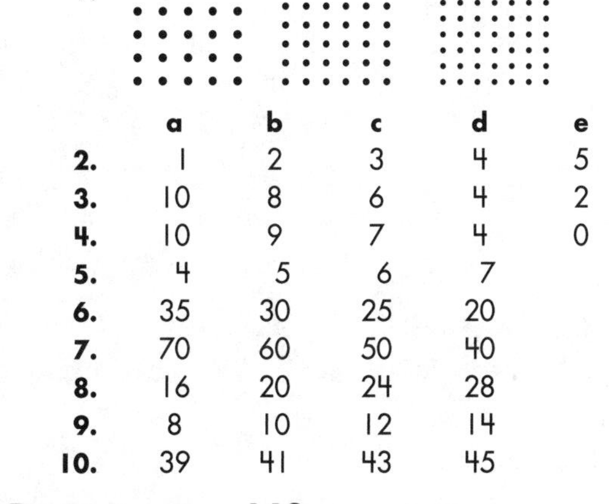

	a	b	c	d	e
2.	1	2	3	4	5
3.	10	8	6	4	2
4.	10	9	7	4	0
5.	4	5	6	7	
6.	35	30	25	20	
7.	70	60	50	40	
8.	16	20	24	28	
9.	8	10	12	14	
10.	39	41	43	45	

Posttest, page 162

	a	b	c
11.			
12.			
13.			

	a	b	c	d
14.	0	4	2	3
15.	3	6	6	3

16. 12 ÷ 6 = □; two
17. 7 × 3 = □; twenty-one
18. 5 + 6 = □; eleven

Final Test

page 163

	a	b	c	d	e
1.	13	22	63	96	61
2.	494	264	179	1310	820
3.	12	35	293	499	398
4.	21	41	1	14	490
5.	6,244	7,068	1,503	8,464	4,057
6.	3,830	4,071	2,583	4,932	3,039
7.	1,881	**8.** 24			

page 164

	a	b	c	d
9.	4,930	59,700	600	700

10a. 500 + 90 + 3 **10b.** 400,000 + 400 + 30

10c. 50,000 + 600 + 3
10d. 5,000 + 900 + 60 + 4 **11a.** 5 < 7
11b. 4 = 4 **11c.** 21 < 27 **11d.** 54 > 51

	a	b	c	d	e
12.	12	260	126	56	122
13.	162	92	65	20	48
14.	8	4	6	3	1
15.	3	5	2	3	5

page 165

16. 81
17. 8

	a	b	c	d
18.	$\frac{3}{4}$	$\frac{1}{2}$	$\frac{5}{8}$	$\frac{1}{10}$
19.	$\frac{1}{2} < \frac{3}{4}$	$\frac{1}{2} = \frac{2}{4}$	$\frac{1}{3} < \frac{1}{2}$	
20.	$\frac{2}{3} < \frac{3}{4}$	$\frac{4}{10} < \frac{4}{8}$	$\frac{1}{2} > \frac{3}{10}$	

page 166

21. 3 in. **22.** 6 cm

	a	b	c
23.	5 m	5 kg	6 g
24.	6 L	3,000 mg	700 cm
25.	20°	52°	0° ; 32°

	a	b	c	d
26.	36 in.	6 ft.	2 pt.	2 gal.
27.	20 qt.	3 qt.	4 c.	24 in.
28.	82 oz.			

page 167

29. 15; 3
30. 75; 3
31. 7 52
32. $8.25; $5.72; $2.53

	a	b
33.	42; 7	18; 8

	a	b	c	d
34.	3:00	3:30	3:15	3:16

35. 11 **36.** 8 **37.** dog **38.** rabbit

page 168

39. Friday **40.** Monday and Thursday **41.** $26
42a. circle; plane **42b.** sphere; solid
42c. rectangular prism; solid **42d.** cylinder; solid

	a	b	c	d
43.	line segment	point	ray	angle
44.	35	40	7	5
45.	3	5	3	7

46. 5 + 2 = □; 7

Notes

Notes